Bend or
BREAK

Bend or BREAK

My Mother's Words, My Life Within Them

Roberta Monroe Keenan

Tate Publishing & *Enterprises*

This novel is a work of fiction. However, several names, descriptions, entities, and incidents included in the story are based on the lives of real people.

The opinions expressed by the author are not necessarily those of Tate Publishing, LLC.

Published by Tate Publishing & Enterprises, LLC
127 E. Trade Center Terrace | Mustang, Oklahoma 73064 USA
1.888.361.9473 | www.tatepublishing.com

Tate Publishing is committed to excellence in the publishing industry. The company reflects the philosophy established by the founders, based on Psalm 68:11,
"The Lord gave the word and great was the company of those who published it."

Book design copyright © 2011 by Tate Publishing, LLC. All rights reserved.
Cover design by Kristen Verser
Interior design by Joel Uber

Published in the United States of America
ISBN: 978-1-61739-779-0
1. Biography & Autobiography; Women
2. Biography & Autobiography; Cultural Heritage
10.12.21

Dedication

I dedicate this writing to the memory of my mother, whose story
this is, to my sisters, Marian and Gayle, and to my brother, James

Acknowledgments

First and foremost, credit belongs to my mother, whose notes and papers form the backbone of this story. Even so, the story would be a mere shadow of itself without the input of my sisters, Marian and Gayle, and my brother, James, who always had time to listen, add their own recollections, and share in the resurrection of often painful memories. Most especially, I thank Marian, who, as first reader and invaluable critic, provided important and incisive analysis of the manuscript-in-progress. Her suggestions and ideas are reflected on many pages. Our cousin, Carol, also proved a valuable source of information and support. And the people at Tate Publishing, thank you! Your expertise, knowledge, and skill were key in bringing this story to life.

Most of all, though, I thank my husband, Jim, who unfailingly supports me, whatever I do, who understands why I don't hear his words when I am emptying a story from my mind into the computer, and who has sustained my life these twenty-seven years.

Prologue

1984

Connie and I are on the road again, going home or, at least trying to. Our annual pilgrimage to Midland, Poseyville and Bullock Creek, once a cause for reunion and laughter, is now a visit to our parents' graves. This year it's also to attend our brother's fiftieth wedding anniversary party.

I am driving. I am always driving. It is always my car, my gasoline, my lunch money. It's enough, Connie says, that she drives from her place to meet me at mine, two hours away—her nerves just won't take the equally long northern trip. And she laughs about it, like she always laughs to fill the air with sound before anyone can respond with disapproval or gloom.

"I wonder if Genevieve is the same," she is saying, speaking of our brother Davis's wife. Connie is referring, not in a kindly way, to Genevieve's eternal niceness, a trait that sometimes proved extremely irritating. There is no putdown for niceness.

"We'll find out," I tell her, and listen to her little peal of laughter, as if I've said something amusing. Most of her banter just flies over my head as I focus on landmarks that will coach me on the next turn.

These little exchanges or non-exchanges make Connie think I'm crabby when I'm only thinking, concentrating, focusing. I sometimes wonder whether she's ever concentrated hard on anything in her life.

I see the intersection ahead where we turn. It's a country crossroad, like any other, I suppose, except that the road is also a log bridge over a deep drainage ditch. That ditch, and others like it, has framed these fields for as long as I can remember. More than one inattentive driver has found herself nose down in these eight-foot-deep canyons. I don't intend to be the next.

The fields here are flat as pancakes, waiting now for farmers to till them again, plant the beans that have thrived here for generations, although they're soy, now, not the Great Northerns I remember. We are almost there.

The anniversary party at the new Grange hall is well-attended. I am glad we came. Davis is so like Pa in many ways, making jokes, smoothing things over, keeping everyone happy. I wish I knew him better. And Genevieve is as nice as ever, to answer Connie's earlier question.

It's mid-afternoon by the time Connie and I leave. At least I didn't have to buy lunch this time—the buffet at the reception was surprisingly good, more than ample for a midday meal and supper combined.

We left flowers on Ma's and Pa's graves before going to the Grange, so now it was only left to return home.

"Let's drive by Crane," Connie says.

From the time I was about two, until I was twelve, we lived in our farm home in Crane.

The house was a pleasant, gable-roofed, cement block house. There was a front porch with white pillars at one end and in front. The part of the house that wasn't block was wood, painted white, and trimmed in light blue. How well I remember that porch, with its cement steps that ended in a good-sized cement slab, a doorstep kind of thing where we chalked abbreviated versions of hopscotch.

From the road, a driveway led beyond the house to the barn and other buildings. Maple trees lined both sides of this drive, making it a shaded and beautiful aisle. There was a barn, granary, a large tool shed—Pa believed tools should be taken care of—and next to that a corn crib, a hog house, a couple of chicken coops. I remember well the cement block outhouse that was later cleaned and remodeled into a smoke house where bacon and hams were cured. A new outhouse of wood was built some distance away where I sometimes sat and speculated about the distasteful methods that must have been required to create the smoke house.

An apple orchard was to one side, in back of the tool shed, in a fenced area where our pigs foraged. I climbed those trees many times to shake down apples for Connie and Ivan and me. It was a race to shimmy down the tree and grab the fallen fruit before the pigs gobbled them up. There were pear trees, too, and a vegetable garden.

How I loved this home place at Crane.

So today, at Connie's urging, we drive the few country miles to find the place again. We know the house is empty now and that the farm buildings are gone. I turn into the driveway and Connie and I sit for a while, seeing that only one maple tree remains beside the driveway and that the orchard beyond is mostly gone. The pillars are missing from the porch and flimsy wood steps replace the solid concrete ones we knew. Someone has built a sleazy railing of wood and braced the porch roof with rough wood props. The worst part–every window we can see is smashed out. Our pretty house has been painted a dreadful yellow brindle and dirt brown. The yard is overgrown with weeds and strewn with old tires and other trash.

We finally get out of the car and walk around the house. The old cellar door is still there, next to broken-down steps that lead to the open kitchen door. We work our way up these steps and peer into the kitchen. Connie decides to go inside, but I can't bring myself to follow. Through the kitchen window I see glass everywhere. Obscene phrases and words are scrawled on the kitchen door and walls. Connie is exploring, gingerly tiptoeing through each room. She says the other rooms are filthy, littered with old mattresses and junk. There are more dirty words, she says, some on every wall.

It seems so dreadful to me, so useless and so pointless. I set my jaw against tears that want to flood my eyes and wait for Connie. We walk silently to the car and I turn the car toward home .

Connie doesn't say much and, for most of the trip, we ride in silence, alone together with our thoughts.

PART ONE

At Home with Ma and Pa

1910

The country village called Crane, a four-corners kind of place between Midland and Poseyville, is still home to me. I think of the school, the neighbors, and most of all, Pa, working the farm and doing his best to keep us all happy. The four of us became five when a new baby, Constance, called Connie, joined Ivan and me the year after we moved there in 1910. Ma had her hands full—she was not a farm wife by nature—and I noticed that she worked faster and faster. When Pa would come in from the barn and Ma would burst into tears with tales of tasks done wrong or half-done, Pa would put his arm around her shoulders and soothe her with words or song. Sometimes he would brush her hair back, kiss her cheek, or try to dance her around the kitchen.

Ma would brush him away, saying things like "That's all fine nonsense for you, Sam, but who's going to churn the butter?"

Besides, dancing around the kitchen wasn't Ma's style. She wanted to go to a real dance and reminded Sam that they hadn't been anywhere in months, due to moving, pregnancy and childbirth. So he promises as soon as Connie is big enough, before winter snows us all in, we will attend a dance. And so it was that we all went to the first Fall Dance at the Grange Hall.

Pa carried the baby and the rest of us walked the quarter-mile from the farm to Crane's four-corners where buildings marked this spot as a town. Standing sentinel at this crossroads were the church, a school, the town hall, and a general store. These buildings weren't as big as our biggest barn, but they seemed pretty big to me. Other, less impressive shops and stores extended like coattails from the town's main four.

The general store was a two-story structure with the store taking up most of the first floor. The store owner and his family lived in the remaining space at the back. Above the store was The Grange Hall, and this was where the dance was being held. We climbed a steep outside stairway to get there. The Grange Hall took up the entire second floor and its varnished expanse stretched before us when Pa opened the door. *Huge*, I thought, remembering that a store and residence shared the same space below. Ma and Pa were members of The Grange and attended a lot of meetings and events here. Pot-luck suppers, plays, and dances were the fun parts—elections and the serious business of the farmers' organization were the others.

The dances were what Ma missed from her unfettered days and what she still cherished and longed for. Pa accepted what he called "Addy's harmless obsession" but it never changed him into a dancer. He would remind us all that he was an actor, musician and singer, not a dancer, and that we could watch him in the plays and watch Ma on the dance floor. Sometimes Pa would join the little group of local farmers-turned-musicians who made music for the dances. While Pa played drums alongside the fiddles and piano, he could himself watch Ma dance.

Ma's dancing was fast and flashy. She found partners among the young and old alike and there were those who observed that she danced with everyone but "the one who brought her." I loved watching Ma flying around, smiling and twirling, making those do-si-do and duck-and-dive moves, but it scared me too, seeing my mother become such a different person. Ma knew every dance that was called, high-stepped to every dance round or square, and never seemed to get the least bit tired like she did at home.

I liked going to the dances, too. There were lots of children...most families didn't have someone to care for them at home. Grandmas, the most likely candidates, were at the party. As the evening wore on, the littlest children and babies, including Connie, would fall asleep on chairs set together as make-shift beds. Ivan and I were too young to join the older children who danced to their hearts' content on their roped-off section of dance floor, so we wandered around, watched Ma dance and ate whatever we wanted from the food table. I knew that Ivan, a few years older than me and always hungry, would stuff his pockets with cookies, crackers and other portable foodstuffs. We weren't supposed to do this, but I never told Pa. Ivan made it clear that I would be sorry if I did.

When the evening finally ended, Pa carried me home. The night was crisp, and the sky was brilliant with stars. Ivan dragged along behind, scuffing his shoes like he wasn't supposed to, and Ma danced on the road ahead of us, holding Connie on her shoulder as she whirled and sang and hummed all the way home.

Chapter Two

For most of the year, the Tittabawassee River flowed peaceably through the center of Midland and westward through the low area called "the flats." It sparkled in the sun and there were parks alongside storefronts and, in some places, flowers and benches. People liked the river, in spite of the havoc its flooding caused almost every spring.

Come spring, when ice broke up and melted, the friendly river changed. It grew taller, wider, and faster, filling its banks and over-flowing into fields and roads. The flats, where houses stood on the same level as the river, flooded first. Houses there might be covered with water to upper story windows, creating a kind of tourist attraction. People came from all over the county to gawk, including us. I remember seeing small chicken coops sailing in the current, sometimes with a chicken on the roof. Boats were sometimes tethered outside upstairs windows.

One version or another of this spectacle happened year after year. People stayed anyway, reading *The Farmers Almanac*, hoping that next year would be different.

In this particular year, the winter had been long and fierce and Pa decided it was time to travel to Midland for supplies. Ma's pantry had been pretty much depleted over the winter and it would be best to refill it before the river flooded. Pa said we would make a day of it and visit Ma's folks. Grandma and Grandpa Cook ran a rooming house in Midland. They had a few boarders, too, but Grandma said she wasn't going to spend all day long cooking, so most of her "guests" ate elsewhere. When we visited we were expected to spend the night, and there never seemed to be a shortage of sleeping rooms.

Ma had baked a cake the day before and fixed two or three other dishes. Pa packed these in the wagon, along with blankets for warmth and pillows for comfort. There was bread, sliced ham, and a jug of water to tide us over until Grandma's. Pa always kept his wagon-fixing tools handy, and he lifted these aboard, harnessed the team to the wagon, and we all piled in. Connie immediately fell asleep among the blankets, and Ivan and I were left to ourselves.

Ivan and I looked at the trees, watched hopefully for returning birds and talked about what we would do in Midland. My eyes kept turning to those deep ditches that lined the road on both sides. Already they were half-full, meaning that major melting had begun. It worried me some, but Pa could see it as well as me, so I kept quiet.

The bridge where we crossed the Tittabawassee was one wide lane of planks on iron, simply a wooden extension of the road with no posts or railings. The bridge was more than wide enough for one wagon, but not for two, and if another driver was coming your way, you just waited until that driver passed. We didn't have to wait today. Crossing the bridge was thrilling in a way. First there was the sound of the horses' hooves against the planks, then the rhythm of wheels against wood and over all the quiet shushing sound of water underneath.

We arrived in Midland in good time and bought the things Ma needed; flour, molasses, and salt among them. She bought cloth to make dresses for Connie and me and some for herself.

We had a fine time window shopping, seeing so many stores with no need to hurry. We weren't going to Grandma Cook's until mid-afternoon. By then, Ma's purchases were securely stowed in crates tied to the wagon, the ham sandwiches were gone and Connie was napping again.

Ivan and I explored Grandma Cook's place while she and Ma visited and worked on the evening meal. At Grandma's, the big meal was always in the evening. Ma said that was because she lived in town.

The room Connie and I stayed in that night had wallpaper with pink roses. I went to sleep thinking about those roses, now only dimly visible in the light from the street lamp.

We started for home early the next morning. One of the boarders had said the river had risen fast overnight, quicker than usual. Someone trying to cross the fast-moving water had been swept away.

The road looked okay at first. Then, not very far ahead, I could see water over the road. We weren't to the bridge yet, the water wasn't very deep and the horses waded easily. Then Pa stopped the horses. Both Ivan and I stood up and looked. The river lay ahead, three times wider than usual. No road to the bridge, no bridge, no road on the other side, nothing but water

Pa got out of the wagon and handed the reins to Ma. He waded to the horses' heads and spoke to them by name, "Now, Nell, now Maude." Pa took hold of Nell's bridle and took a step forward. For a moment, the team hesitated and Nell gave a low, snoring whicker that might have been a question.

"Come," Pa said, and they did, into water higher than their knees, moving slowly, with Pa feeling for footing as he led. I could see the water rising on the wagon wheels and hear the water whirling past. The taste in my mouth felt like fear, and I swallowed, hard, but I knew Pa would get us through.

It seemed forever before the noise of the water was behind us and Pa was guiding the horses between those deep ditches I knew were under the water on either side of the road. When finally the road was fully visible again, Pa stopped the team. I heard him saying something to Nell and Maude and saw him rub each horse's nose before coming back to the wagon.

Pa took the reins from Ma, who looked at him without speaking.

"The good Lord was watching over us today, Addy," he said. Pa put his arm around Ma, pulled her to his side. They stayed like that the rest of the way home.

Chapter Three

Our days were like beads of a necklace, marking the months and seasons. From spring floods to planting, greening to harvest, and from canning to north winds and snow that melted into spring floods, life circled round. It was comfortable and predictable, or so I thought.

Then I entered school at Crane. Pa said we were lucky to have this school and a teacher to teach us and that we were to do our best. School was not just an opportunity, it was a duty.

My first day at school was going to be fun, I thought, not knowing that I was in for a shock. Miss Fromm, a stick-thin woman with puffy hair, rang her bell to signify silence. She said we were each to stand and give our full name. When it was my turn, I stood and said, in my loudest six-year-old voice, "Amelia Lorraine Whitlock." She asked if I was called "Amy." When I said, "Yes, ma'am," in my more normal, timid voice, she gave me a little smile and nodded. I liked my name and liked the way it had sounded when spoken aloud. I thought Miss Fromm liked it too.

But after every student's name was recited, she showed us her fair whip…a miniature buggy whip with a handle, long flexible body and a lash at the end. Her thin arm jerked out and the whip cut the air with a small whistling sound. If anyone had been whispering before, they were silent now as the teacher outlined the rules. The fair whip, she said, would hang on a nail behind the bookcase, ready to use if rules were breached. I had never been whipped, or spanked. Pa might speak in his hard voice, or Ma might jerk me by one arm, but I was never hit. Pa didn't even believe in whipping the horses, and this teacher was going to whip us kids.

Miss Fromm did apply the whip, usually to bigger boys who just wouldn't settle down, or who said things she didn't like. One time she used her whip on my brother Ivan, striking him across his shoulders while he sat. I can still recall Ivan's dark look, the way his eyes flashed, and the words he said later, "She better not do that again." Miss Fromm never whipped me but when she lashed any student I was certain I was going to be next. I guess I thought I must be guilty of something.

Ivan and I walked the short distance to school. In the winter this was a cold walk, down the middle of the road after a new snow fall, or balancing on the ridges of snow eventually plowed to the side. Either way, we were cold when we arrived and the school was often cold too. The stove, with its long overhead stovepipe that spanned the full length of the classroom, provided enough heat. The problem was that Miss Fromm was not an early riser and sometimes when school was supposed to begin, the fire would just be kindling, the inkwells still frozen solid. I knew the failure rested with Miss Fromm because I knew that Pa or Ma would always be up an hour or two before us children to fire up the wood stove. Miss Fromm had no such concern for the children in her charge and I, fearing the whip, said nothing.

Reading was an adventure and a door into new worlds. I quickly covered the beginner's reader "Mama Loves Baby, Baby Loves Mama" and started on others. With students ages five to sixteen and textbooks for all, there was a wonderful assortment available. With the advantage of knowing how to read before school, my progress was good. Somehow, I thrived in this school, perhaps because of, perhaps in spite of Miss Fromm.

When Miss Fromm's contract was not renewed for the following year, I wasn't particularly sorry to see her go. I didn't know why she left but fancied it was because someone told about those unnecessarily cold mornings. I wondered if Ivan had found a way to get even for that whipping.

A later teacher, Mr. Goyette, lived in LaPorte and drove his horse and buggy to Crane on Monday, boarded during the week, and went back to LaPorte Friday. He didn't threaten us with fair whips or other physical punishment. His disciplinary tool was constant criticism. Why was I sitting like that? Why was this paper smudged? The criticism was mostly lavished on the boys and us younger girls. He pampered the older girls, letting them boss us around and do more or less as they pleased. When I finally gathered up enough courage to complain about one of big girls, he just laughed.

Pa was a director of the school and so, I suppose, shared responsibility for hiring teachers. I wondered if I complained to him, would it make a difference or would I just be a tattle-tale? I kept quiet.

I was a fifth grader now, but Pa still brought lunch for Ivan, Connie and me most every day. These were tasty hot meals from home, while most other students ate from lunch pails with cold sandwiches. We got teased about this sometimes, about being spoiled babies, and sometimes I wished Pa would stop. Mr. Goyette had another take on it. He hinted that Pa was spying on him, coming to school just to take a look-see. I didn't tell Pa.

One February day, Pa got a letter threatening to burn down the school. The letter was signed with the inked imprint of a black hand. Pa called a directors meeting and learned that other directors had received similar threats. The chief suspect was Mr. Goyette, and he was sent to Midland to have his writing compared to the writing on the letters. Nothing came of that, except that Mr. Goyette's temper was not improved. He was more critical than ever and more suspicious.

One day, early morning, while school was in session, I was gazing around and looked at the ceiling near the bell rope, and noticed fire burning there. A couple of the big boys quickly climbed into the belfry and put the fire out. Everyone felt threatened now, and I took my books home every night lest they get burned up. Then, one icy snowy night in March, the school building caught fire and burned to the ground. This was the first night I had not brought my books home, so away went the books.

Classes were resumed in the old Methodist church, now empty and boarded up. Somewhere desks were found, windows un-boarded, and school went on as usual. Then came other threatening notes. One read, "If you don't get the damn kids out of the church, we'll burn it too."

Not too long after that, I went to school to find kerosene had been poured on a church pew in the rear of the building and a small fire there had burned itself out. This time Pa was told and another directors meeting held. Even so, nothing happened, and the school term wore on.

Mr. Goyette seemed more defiant now, late many days and later on Mondays. His punctuality policy was definitely a do-as-I-say-not-as-I-do standard. The former church caretaker, seeing how things were going, took it upon himself to open the school and get the stove going most mornings.

When the school year ended and Mr. Goyette left one last time for LaPorte, there was no farewell party. I heard Pa say, shaking his head in disbelief, that Mr. Goyette had found a young woman in LaPorte to be his wife and that he had taken a new teaching job in Indiana. We were shut of him for good.

Chapter Four

The sound of Ma's voice woke me. Connie and I were sleeping in our upstairs bedroom. Ivan was in the next room. I slipped from beneath the covers and tiptoed to the floor grate that let heat rise into our bedroom from the stove below. I had learned long ago that this grate was also a secret window into the downstairs hall outside Ma's and Pa's bedroom.

"I just can't do this, Sam," Ma was saying, her voice filled with tears and panic. Pa shushed her.

"Hush, Addy, you'll raise the house." Ma was crying and I imagined from the muffled sound that her face was pressed into a pillow.

My own heart was beating fast and I shivered. By now, Connie was awake, too, sleepy and stumbling from bed. I put my finger to my lips and beckoned. I hugged her close as we waited for further news.

I heard Pa trying to comfort Ma, saying things like "We'll get by," and "Things will look better in the morning," words that only made Ma cry harder.

Then the night was quiet, and I thought the talk was over when Ma spoke. Her voice was steady now, calm.

"I don't want another baby, Sam, I can't do it. My hands are full already. Don't you think three children are enough?" Her question unanswered, she continued, "I won't do it, Sam. I'm not going through with it. I'll get Mrs. Kettner…"

"You'll do nothing of the kind." That was Pa's hard voice. In the quiet that followed, I knew Pa was measuring what words to use next.

"If you need help, Addy, we'll get help. But there's nothing we will do about the other. If it's meant to be, it will be. And that's all I have to say."

That's how I learned that a baby was coming. I hoped Ma would say something to Ivan and Connie and me about it, but she didn't. She just grew bigger and bigger until one day Pa took all of us children to Aunt Lorraine's for a visit.

"It'll be a few days," Pa told us. "When you come back home, you'll have a new sister or brother." And that's all he had to say about that.

Aunt Lorraine was Pa's sister, and we visited there often. The farm where she and Uncle Al lived was bigger than ours, and so was the house. No one had to double-up, there were so many bedrooms, but Connie wouldn't let me have a room to myself. If put in a separate room, she would cry and cry until Aunt Lorraine would say that it looked like I would just have to share with Connie. After all, she would say, you share a room at home. That was her reason for sharing now but it was my reason for not sharing now. Was I never to have my own space even when space was plentiful? But I never said any such thing to Aunt Lorraine and Connie slept quietly with me.

Aunt Lorraine's kitchen was my favorite room. It was large, with two separate cook stoves, a sink where you could pump water, and a large butcher block table where Aunt Lorraine prepared most dishes. She baked six loaves of bread at a time and worked all morning to ready the big noon meal. More than a

dozen places were set at the long dining room table and sometimes extras were added, depending on who showed up. Besides
Aunt Lorraine's own four children, there was Uncle Al, Ivan,
Connie, and me, and three or four farm helpers, mostly cousins
or other relatives. There was a lot of food on that table but those
who arrived late still might go away hungry. Aunt Lorraine's
bunch had big appetites.

We were at Aunt Lorraine's for about a week before Pa showed
up with the team and wagon. It was time to go home. While we
got our things together, Pa talked with Aunt Lorraine and waited
while his sister dished up a crock of beef stew, wrapped a loaf of
bread and boxed a cake to send with us. I marveled at all this food
to share when she hadn't even known what day Pa was coming.

We didn't get the news until we were on our way. As the horses
pulled the wagon toward home, Pa told us that there was a new
baby brother at home.

"We've named him Davis Samuel," Pa said, "after Grandpa
Cook and your Pa." Grandpa Davis Cook was Ma's own father.

"You'll need to help your Ma," Pa said to me. "She's not real
strong yet. I'm asking you to help out as much as possible. And
that means you, too," he added, nodding toward Ivan and Connie. Connie's eyes grew big and her head bobbed in eager agreement. Ivan was not so pleased, judging by his shrug and the way
he turned his eyes to the passing scenery.

As the summer faded into fall, it seemed to me that Ma was
fading too. Davis, or Davey, as we called him, was growing. Ma
fretted that she didn't have enough milk to nurse him. Pa bought
bottles and showed me how to mix milk, syrup and some other
ingredients for Davey's food. I thought it tasted awful, but he
drank it right down.

Ma was having trouble with her hands. She developed a rash
that itched and bled, and the doctor called it eczema. Pa said she
should quit wringing her hands so much. Ma cried a lot and said

she couldn't clean or use soaps. She couldn't knead the bread. Pa bought Ma a pair of rubber gloves and hired a neighbor lady to do the wash. Ivan and I were assigned to dishwashing. I helped knead the bread.

One day after bottle feeding Davey and patting him to sleep, I came into the kitchen to see Ma sitting at the table and crying. She had her sewing basket on the table and was trying to mend a torn rubber glove with needle and thread.

Alarmed, I ran to the fields where Pa and Ivan were working. He left Ivan there and I followed him back to the house. Pa put Ma to bed, threw the gloves in the trash, and went back to the fields. He told me not to leave the baby and Connie alone in the house again. *Alone?*, I thought. *I didn't leave them alone. Ma was there.*

When school started, things got worse. Ma was by herself now with Davey, while Ivan, Connie, and I were in school. I could see Pa was getting worn out, trying to run both the house and farm, and I worried that I would be asked to leave school for Ma's sake.

One Saturday I was in the kitchen with Ma and she was looking out the window, toward the road. She was wringing her hands again.

"Amy, come quick," she said, and I did, coming up beside her and following her gaze with my eyes. "See that?"

"See what, Ma, I don't see anything."

"Out there, on the electric wires. The skeletons. Those skeletons, all thin bones, balancing and dancing on those wires. They've been there all week, off and on. Tell me you see them, too."

Ma's eyes pleaded with me, asked me for assurance. She looked so scared. There was no choice but to see what she saw. I told her I saw those bony skeletons, and they were going away soon. I said she should sit down and we should have some tea, and the baby is crying, and Pa will know what to do, just wait, Pa will be coming in from the barn soon. We waited. Both Ma and I were basket cases that day.

Chapter Five

Uncle George and Aunt Mary came to get Davey and his things. They wrapped him in a blanket and carried him away to their farm at Bullock Creek. Davey didn't seem to mind, but I cried, not wanting this new baby brother to be taken away.

"It's only for a while," Pa said. "When Ma comes home from the hospital, Davis will come home, too."

Uncle George was Pa's older brother. He and Aunt Mary were very religious or, as Pa put it, "they take their religion seriously." Without children of their own they had taken in several children over the years, mostly sons and daughters of relatives facing some misfortune or another. It was their Christian duty, Uncle George said, and I suppose it was, but I thought it wouldn't be much fun being someone's Christian duty.

Ma hadn't gone to the hospital yet. She stayed in the bedroom, mostly, waiting for Pa to do something. The plan was for Uncle Al to bring his buggy and drive Ma and Pa to the train station at Midland. From there, Pa would stay with Ma during the long train ride to the west side of the state. Once Ma was delivered to the hospital, Pa would come back to us.

I asked Pa why Ma couldn't just be at the hospital at Midland and he said it was not the right kind of hospital. The doctor had decided that Traverse City State Hospital was the proper place.

I learned later that some people called this place "the nuthouse," but I didn't know that then.

When the day came for Ma to go, Pa helped her dress, and I helped brush her hair. Ma had always been so energetic, so busy and so wound up. Now she seemed limp and without energy. She told us all "good-bye", smiled a wan smile and waved her gloved hand from the buggy. Connie and I were crying. Ivan just turned away and ran out to the barn.

Aunt Lorraine had come with Uncle Al to watch the three of us until Uncle Al returned from Midland. Then we would all go to Aunt Lorraine's where we would stay until Pa returned.

It didn't take long for the news to get around the community. A day or so after Pa came back and took us home; several Grange wives brought hot meals. People wanted to help. The wash was already hired out, but Pa said we could do the regular things, like sweeping and dusting. It worked for awhile, until the neighbor ladies had furnished all their best casseroles and charity got old. Then Pa hired a housekeeper. Or, should I say, he hired a string of housekeepers.

The first, a Mrs. Beeman, had two sons, Ian, about Connie's age, and Peter, who was Ivan's age. Peter stayed with the Harmons, a family across the road, so we didn't have to put up with him, but we did have to put up with Ian. Mrs. Beeman said we picked on Ian and were mean to him. Maybe we did and maybe we were, but I don't think we hurt him much. But Mrs. Beeman complained to Pa and we got punished. Pa, who never believed in whipping the horses, took his razor strop to me and to Ivan. Not once, but several times. Ivan and I were both glad when Pa finally sent her away.

Mrs. McAllister came next, with her little boy, Johnny. What Mrs. McAllister didn't like to do was work. Every afternoon she took a nap, and woe to anyone who woke her. One good thing about Mrs. McAllister was that every week or so she would go home to Midland for a few days. She lived in what Pa called, "Paddy Hollow," the closest thing Midland had to a slum.

One day Mrs. McAllister told Connie and me to come upstairs with her and she would get some postcards for us to look at. We waited while she searched for the cards in her trunk. Then I saw something of mine in her trunk, a bottle of Heliotrope perfume in a little wooden case, that my teacher had given me. When Pa came in that evening, I found a minute to tell him. He listened and when Mrs. McAllister went home in a few days, he searched the trunk. Pa found some of Ivan's shirts and pants, two kimonos of Ma's, and several other small items and knick-knacks. Pa took them all out, took the trunk to Mrs. McAllister's, and that was the end of her.

Then Mrs. Smithson came from Frederic.

Chapter Six

We all went to meet Mrs. Smithson at the train station in Midland. I dreaded the meeting and didn't hold much hope for this one, considering what we'd already seen.

I saw her alight from the train and knew she was different. A boy came off the train ahead of her, took her hand as she stepped down to the platform. This boy, we would learn, was her son, Jessup. He was about Ivan's age and would stay at the Harmon farm across the road, as Peter had done.

Mrs. Smithson was tall, taller than Ma anyway. She was slender but not thin, and wore a crisp bonnet trimmed with silk flowers. From beneath the bonnet, dark, shiny hair blossomed around her face. Her dress, dark and soft-looking, appeared unwrinkled and dust free, and how could that be after such a long trip?

Pa introduced us children and she took our hands one by one, smiled into each face and said our names.

When her trunk and Jessup's case were loaded on the wagon, we all climbed in and Pa turned the team toward home. I noticed that Jessup offered his hand to steady his mother's step up. At that moment, I must admit, I was captivated by Mrs. Smithson.

At supper the next evening, while we all sat around the dining table and sampled Mrs. Smithson's cooking, she suddenly pushed her chair back and stood up. Everyone stopped eating. My own fork was poised midway.

"I think I'll eat in the kitchen," she said, and without ceremony, picked up her plate and left.

"What happened, Pa?" I wanted to know.

Pa seemed equally baffled but left the table himself to find out.

When Pa returned, he told us that Mrs. Smithson found our table manners "unappetizing," especially using fingers instead of proper utensils, speaking with our mouths full, and neglecting to cut food into smaller portions before eating. I was embarrassed and burst into tears. Ivan said nothing and, finished with the pork chop he had been gnawing, dropped the bone on his plate. Connie said, "I can use a spoon," and stood on her chair to take a spoon from their common jar.

I had no idea our table manners needed improvement. We hadn't been criticized before, not by Ma, Grandma, Aunt Lorraine, or any of the housekeepers and that seemed like approval to me. Mrs. Smithson thought otherwise. She introduced napkins to the table, squares cut from feed sacks, and hemmed on Ma's sewing machine, and taught us how to use them.

Beyond manners, Mrs. Smithson set everyday tasks for Ivan, Connie, and me. We were expected to do them and she made sure we did. She corrected our English when we misused words.

There was something about the way she did these things that made Connie and I want to please her. Ivan was less compliant, but he grudgingly followed. One time I saw Mrs. Smithson put her hand on Ivan's shoulder and speak directly into his face, but she never slapped any of us. She never tattled to Pa.

Some months after her arrival, Mrs. Smithson said she wanted freedom to travel by herself. This was somewhat shocking to me. When Ma was home, she never went anywhere without Pa. When Pa and Ma traveled without us kids, they used a lightweight one-horse buggy now stored in the barn. Otherwise, we used the larger wagons.

Pa got the buggy from storage, cleaned and waxed its leather and brass, and allowed that it was for Mrs. Smithson's use, along with our regular buggy horse. Mrs. Smithson—Pa now called her Rosalie—was now free to travel to Crane, on to Midland, or anywhere she chose. Pa would harness the horse sometimes, but Mrs. Smithson knew how to do it herself, and often did.

Besides her son, Jessup, Mrs. Smithson had a daughter, Catherine, who attended high school in Midland and boarded there. After graduating, she planned to attend nursing school at Hurley Hospital in Flint. With the horse and buggy at her disposal, Mrs. Smithson could visit Catherine more often. She brought Catherine to our place during school breaks and holidays.

About the same time that Mrs. Smithson began driving the buggy, she had her piano shipped from Frederic. The furniture in the living room was adjusted to make space. At first the piano looked strange there, so large and shiny, like a rose among zinnias. After a few days, somehow, it was as if it had always been there. Mrs. Smithson played in the evenings and everyone sang. Sometimes Pa would sing in his rich baritone voice while Mrs. Smithson played. Other times she sang with him in her clear soprano voice.

Life on the farm was much improved. It seemed like Mrs. Smithson could do just about anything. She always had some sewing project going and the dresses Connie and I wore were most often garments she made for us. The year I changed schools to begin seventh grade, I wore a most elegant coat that Mrs. Smithson had fashioned for me from one of her own.

Sometime during the first year, I contracted typhoid fever. Catherine took care of me, honing her nursing skills, I suppose. I was moved to a downstairs bedroom and Catherine slept there with me. Fresh air was considered vital to my recovery and every night the window stood wide-open to the freezing night air. I ran a high fever, my hair loosened and much of it was combed out. This was a grave wound to my vanity, especially when what remained was cut short. As I recovered, I was allowed to sit up more each day—and the best part—sit at the table with the family. I sat in a rocking chair, bolstered with blankets and pillows, feeling really babied and liking it.

No one else got the disease, not even Catherine, and I wondered why I got what everyone knew was a filth disease. Whatever the cause, it was never discussed.

The second summer she was with us, Mrs. Smithson asked if I would like to go on a summer visit. She and I went to Frederic on the train where she left me with her parents. Their life in town was quite different from life on the farm. We dressed up a lot, went to church and parties, and no one ever raised their voice or broke things. This was a wonderful time for me, and I wished it would never end. It did, of course, and I returned home without realizing I had completed Mrs. Smithson's version of charm school.

When I came back to the farm in late summer, Pa had bought a car. It was a tinny thing, less substantial looking than the buggy, and only good when roads were dry and scraped. Pa took a great deal of pleasure in this new gadget though, and we went to Midland more often. Watching the way that Mrs. Smithson studied Pa while he was driving, I knew it was only a matter of time until she would be behind the wheel.

At first Pa resisted, saying women weren't meant to drive automobiles, but that was a silly excuse to Mrs. Smithson, and I knew she would get her way. She told Pa she would drive in the field until she got it figured out and away she went. It wasn't long before she was back, on foot. She had tried to take the car through the barnyard to the field and got mired there. It took Nell and Maude only minutes to free the light vehicle and Pa said the horses were laughing about it. Mrs. Smithson was not amused.

One day I walked into the kitchen and saw Pa and Mrs. Smithson kissing. They saw me and pulled away, laughing. Later, when Mrs. Smithson and I were sitting at the piano together, I asked her about it. She looked at me, not seeming surprised at my question, but more as if appraising my expression. I was shocked at what she said.

"Your Pa thinks he wants to marry me." She was looking directly at me in her usual way. Her voice was serious and quiet but I could see the way her lips pursed and how one side of her mouth quirked in the way it did when she disapproved of something.

I wanted to say more. I thought, *My Pa's married already. What about Ma?* Instead, I said nothing, as was my habit. After a moment, Mrs. Smithson reached out, squeezed my hand, and began playing the piano. The tune she played was *Love's Old Sweet Song*.

Chapter Seven

Pa sent me to a new school for seventh grade. Eight grades were taught at Crane, but Pa said I needed a change. He didn't like it that my homework was finished before supper and said the world was a bigger place than Crane, and I should see a bit of it. This school wasn't in a city, exactly, but it wasn't country, either. It was two stories tall and made of brick. A grand belfry held a very large bell whose periodic clanging dictated our schedule. There must have been at least a hundred students, none below grade seven. Like me, they came from other schools. There were two girls from my old school at Crane but we pretended not to know each other. We had joined a bigger world.

The school was some miles south, some place between Owosso and Ovid. For more exact directions, you would have had to ask Pa. What I knew was that it was too far for daily transport. I don't know why Pa chose this school in particular. I never asked him and he never said.

As was customary, I boarded with a family there and walked to school. My upstairs room contained a single bed, dresser and straight back chair. By pulling out one dresser drawer part way and putting a board across it, I had a makeshift desk where I did my homework. It was cold in the winter, but I was used to that.

The older couple who lived here, Mr. and Mrs. Johnson, had sold their farm and moved into this smaller place. Neither talked to me much, seldom more than "Good morning," "Supper's ready," and "Time for bed." They seemed to walk through each day as if half-asleep. Mr. Johnson coughed more than he talked, a dry, hacking noise that was loud enough to wake me if it happened in the night. But even that sound, after a while, became part of my routine, rather than a disturbance to it.

The sum total of what I learned about the Johnsons that whole year wouldn't have filled the space on the back of an envelope. The good side of all this passivity was that they left me alone. Mrs. Johnson didn't expect me to help with housework. She made my bed, a luxury to be enjoyed, packed my lunch, and accepted my comings and goings without comment.

School was hard with homework every day. The books were varied and exciting. I was fascinated with tales of scientific expeditions, Hottentots and hunts for jungle animals. We studied the human body and I memorized the names of all the bones, even though I didn't have to. The Johnsons owned books, too, and I read these at night. Mrs. Johnson never blinked an eye at my selections from her shelf but I worried, sometimes, that Pa would object if he knew. So I kept quiet and just soaked up the words. I was too busy studying to make friends.

Ever so often I would get to go home for holidays and school breaks. The Johnsons would drive me halfway and Pa would meet us and take me the rest of the way

That first spring, after the snow was gone and the roads dry, Mrs. Smithson came to meet me instead of Pa. She was wearing her flowered hat and looked all dressed up. The horse and buggy awaited.

"Where's Pa?" She didn't answer immediately. Instead, she embraced me and began to walk toward the buggy. I followed.

"I wanted to come, today," she said. "I wanted to tell you myself."

We climbed into the buggy and took a moment to straighten our skirts. I didn't think I wanted to know what she wanted to tell me herself, so I kept silent.

"I've decided that it's time for me to return to Frederic."

I could never have imagined such terrible news. Worse than terrible. Disastrous. Tears began to drizzle down my cheeks.

"It's just time for me to go," she repeated. "My brother is coming Sunday. I've already packed the trunk, and he's bringing a wagon for the rest. Of course, Jessup will go, too.

"There's one other thing, Amy. I'm leaving the piano. I know how much you enjoy it and you've done well with your lessons, so I'm leaving it for you."

There were words I wanted to say, but they were all jumbled up. One or two words leaked out, but they made no sense and I strangled the others back. Tears no longer drizzled, they poured. Mrs. Smithson offered me her handkerchief. It was a soft, flowered thing and smelled of her perfume.

When we arrived at Crane and stepped from the buggy, Mrs. Smithson extended her hand, palm up, and I knew she wanted her handkerchief. She meant to spare me the chore that good manners required, of washing, ironing, and returning a used hanky. I dropped the sodden ball into her hand.

Sometime during the trip, Mrs. Smithson had given me a small box. "Stationery," she said, "and stamps. Write to me in Frederic."

I had no intention of writing. She had quit us, quit Pa, and Ivan and Connie and me. For no reason, or no reason I knew, she had just walked out after two years, leaving us high and dry. We had trusted her, counted on her and yes, loved her. I loved her.

When Mrs. Smithson's brother came to take her and her things away from us, I stayed in my room. I heard her come to my door and say, "Good bye, Amy, I'm leaving now. Take good care of yourself and Connie." Then she was gone.

Chapter Eight

May 23, 1919

Dear Mrs. Smithson,

I am writing to say we are well. Connie has been making trouble in school by showing off and tossing tantrums. Ivan pinches her when she does this at home, saying it will straighten her out but it doesn't really work. I would never dare do this myself. Connie would just yell worse and run tell Pa. I have finished school for the term and my grades were good, except for math. I am learning algebra and there will be more next term.

We don't have a housekeeper now. Grandma Cook stays here a lot and Mrs. Ambrose is still doing the wash. Pa says we can get along.

Pa says he misses your piano playing in the evenings. I am practicing almost every day I'm home and doing the exercises you taught me. Thank you for leaving us your piano.

Hope you are well and happy.

Yours truly,

Amelia Lorraine Whitlock

P.S. I miss you.

The letter looked nice with its blue ink bright against cream paper, but that's not the reason I wrote it. I felt miserable and guilty over the way I acted when she left. Maybe this letter would help make up for that.

I thought about Ma a lot that spring. She had been gone almost three years now. During that time I had seen her only twice, once when she came home for a short visit the first year, and once when Pa took us to Traverse City. Once in a while we would get to see our baby brother, Davey, too, but Uncle George and Aunt Mary weren't exactly welcoming when we would visit. Davey called them Mama and Daddy, and I didn't like that one bit. All we had of Davey, really, was a photograph of us children taken when a traveling photographer came to town. We were all dressed up and Aunt Mary saw that Davey was dressed up too when we stopped by their farm to pick him up. I held Davey on my lap that whole trip. Then we took him back to Aunt Mary's house.

Pa assured us that Ma would come home one day. The doctor said she could come home whenever she wanted. All she had to do was write a letter to Pa, saying she wanted to come home.

When I wasn't away at school, I picked up the mail most days. Our mailbox was right in front of the house, and I would watch for the mailman to come by. I kept hoping for a letter from Ma. I couldn't understand why she wouldn't just come home when no one was making her stay. This thought didn't make me feel real kindly toward Ma and not too good about myself.

One day the letter came. I took it from the mailbox and ran to the barn where Pa was working with the horses. I could hardly wait for him to open it. Pa read it aloud. It was short of amenities, or words of affection. All it said was "Sam, when can you come get me? I've been here long enough. Addy."

Pa brought Ma home on the train while Ivan, Connie, and I waited at home with Grandma Cook. We were all on the porch when Uncle Al drove up with Ma, Pa, and her small valise.

I hardly recognized Ma. She was little more than skin and bones and her once plentiful hair was thin and dull. She would have been the first to observe that her dress wasn't fit for the rag bag, ill-fitting and wrinkled as it was. Her teeth were discolored or missing and she walked with a limp. I could hardly believe this wreck of a woman was my mother.

Grandma Cook was speechless. She just wrapped her arms around Ma and then walked her into the house, holding her arm the whole time.

That day passed, and weeks, too. Ma settled in and Pa took many trips with her to Midland to get her teeth fixed. A dressmaker came and measured Ma for dresses, gowns, and nightwear. Pa said it was because the clothes she had were out of style, but I knew how they hung on her thinner frame. Yet, over the summer, she began to look better and sound more like herself. She gained a little weight and fussed about the effect this would have on her new dresses.

Every day I brushed Ma's hair. She was so weak that even this effort tired her out at first. When she got stronger, I just kept doing it. Brushing was supposed to be good for your hair, and I hoped so. Lots of hair came out on the brush at first, and I worried that she might lose what hair she had. One day as I was brushing and brushing, and she was watching in the mirror, she said to me, with a little of the familiar edge to her voice, "This is what a diet of prison food does for you." I kept brushing.

It was decided that Davey would come home. Davey walked in that day, holding Aunt Mary's hand, and looked around with smiles and curiosity. He came right to me and I picked him up, quite a weight now at four years old. Davey called me Ammel, a short version of Amelia. Aunt Mary believed in using full names, not nicknames like "Amy," and I was amused that all this insistence had brought was another nickname.

Ma watched Davey bouncing around. She was nervous again, twisting her hands, trying to smile. When she finally decided to pick him up, Davey looked startled and began to cry. He squirmed and kicked and yelled and Ma couldn't soothe him. Uncle George and Aunt Mary had been standing near the door all this time, saying little. Now Aunt Mary went to Ma and plucked Davey from her arms. In a moment he was quiet, leaning on her shoulder. "Mama," he said.

Ma turned away and looked out the window. Pa fixed tea, and I brought out cookies Ma had baked the day before. Uncle George and Aunt Mary finally sat down.

It was then that Ma said to Aunt Mary, "I think you should take Davis back with you. I'm a stranger to him. You're his folks now."

So Davey went back with Uncle George and Aunt Mary.

Later that night I heard Ma crying. She was telling Pa, "I told you I couldn't do it. I can't do it. I won't do it."

Davey stayed with Uncle George and Aunt Mary until he was grown. We saw him sometimes in the summer and for photograph taking. Many years later, when all of us were middle-aged, Davey voiced his bitterness. He said he was effectively disinherited because Uncle George believed his inheritance should come from Pa. Pa believed he would inherit from Uncle George, who was much better off.

I told Davey I was sorry and I was sure Ma and Pa would be sorry too, if they were alive.

Chapter Nine

While I was away studying eighth grade, Pa sold the farm at Crane. He told me during Christmas holidays, giving me the worst Christmas gift I never wanted. I loved our place at Crane with all its buildings, trees, and fields. The barns, the chicken coops, the orchards…all held precious memories. This was our rock-solid, permanent home. Now we were to be yanked from our land like weeds, uprooted for replanting someplace unknown. Pa said we had until spring plowing to find another place and move.

One evening, when we were all in the kitchen, cleaning up after supper, I asked Pa why he sold the farm. He said the reasons were between him and Ma and that they were of no concern to me. "But this is my home," I insisted. "How can you just do this?" His response was an arrow to my heart.

"You are being overly headstrong, Amelia, and it's not very attractive. I have said why the choice was made. Remember your place." He turned away and said to Ma, "I'll be in the barn."

Ma was still washing dishes. "Why, Ma? Can you say?"

"Let's just say that there's nothing left here for us, now. Pa wasn't re-elected school director. All we get are snubs from our former friends at the Grange. Whispers and snide remarks about the nuthouse. Davis not coming home. We need a fresh start."

She dried her hands on her apron. "And Amy, like your Pa said, it's not good to develop headstrong ways. Try to be more adaptable to events. Bend or break, Amy. Learn to bend so you don't break. You know what happened to me." She was looking directly at me. There was a tear in her eye, and I had to look away.

The farm Pa found was in Dansville, a small town about 75 miles south and west of Crane. The house was a big clapboard thing, lots of cold rooms and drafty windows. The barn had been newly repainted, and a new lock put on the tool shed, while rust stained the kitchen sink and faded wallpaper set the mood in every room. Ma said it would only take a little elbow grease to turn the place around.

Houses were closer together here than at Crane. The pastures and tillable lands extended behind the house instead of on either side. I had my own upstairs room, as did Ivan and Connie, and there were rooms left over. Pa and Ma slept downstairs, in a big bedroom next to the parlor where the piano stood. All the rooms were bigger than in the house at Crane, but where that house was solid and firmly planted, this one seemed lightly tethered and apt to be blown away by the first cyclone that whirled by.

I began high school at Dansville. Now I lived at home again, a mixed blessing, for I was a part of all those day-to-day exchanges and friction that come with family living. I was reminded every day how demanding farm living could be, every action timed by animals, the seasons, the harvest. Pa and Ma worked constantly and hard—their life was never easy. Ma said I should go to Normal School and learn to be a school teacher. There was a teacher's school in the county, and Ma said they could afford to send me there. So I studied throughout high school. I joined the debating team and found friends there. Mostly, I read and studied. My reward was graduating a year early as valedictorian and being accepted at Ingham County Normal School. I was seventeen years old, and Ma was proud of me.

By now, Ivan had finished school too and moved to Lansing to "find his fortune." Pa had expected Ivan's help on the farm and was not happy with this desertion. Ma said Ivan needed to find himself.

Connie was beginning high school and was not much of a student. Her major assets were a pretty face, small rounded figure, and hair that was naturally wavy. Connie had lots of friends and spent most of her time getting ready to go places with this one or that one. That tinkling laugh of hers attracted people like a magnet. Pa called her a social butterfly, always with a twinkle and a smile of approval. He might not have been so amused had he seen the way Connie tucked the top of her skirt under the waistband to raise the hem several inches, or when she colored her lips and cheeks with rouge most likely filched from the Five and Ten.

So Connie sailed into high school like a princess on a parade float while I marched into teacher's college like a drab soldier in the war for independence.

Teacher's college was surprisingly easy. The techniques were simple to learn and, thanks to my bookworm days, I had already done much of the reading. An emphasis was placed on handwriting, and teaching students the "correct" way to write. Thus I earned a certificate in The Palmer Method of Handwriting, a discipline I inflicted on hundreds of students over the years. After a year's schooling, I had my teacher's certificate.

That summer Connie and I were allowed to attend the Ingham County Fair at the city of Mason, the county seat, about eight miles from Dansville. Pa reminded me to keep an eye on Connie—I being the more responsible.

The fair was colorful and noisy, with its merry-go-round, Ferris Wheel, and side shows. Of course there were farm exhibits, and we hit those first, knowing that Pa would ask about the sheep and hogs, and which breeds of chickens were shown. Best to get that obligation out of the way before exploring the midway.

Connie and I had just bought ice creams and were taking in the sights along the way when two young men walked over.

"Hello," one of them said, "Want to go on the Ferris Wheel?"

"Yes, sure," said Connie, letting her magnet laugh tinkle forth.

"Wait," I wanted to say, but didn't and next thing you know we were on the Ferris Wheel.

The two introduced themselves as Colby "Call me Cole" Morgan and Wesley Ford. Cole sat by me and Wes, as he preferred to be called, sat by Connie, four of us in one car. I looked at their shoes. Both wore the kind of leather boots associated with outdoor work and farming, "work shoes" Pa called them. They were clean, not polished, no one polishes work shoes, and that's what I noted. No barn remains clung to their shoes, no manure, no straw, no mud or muck. That was a good omen.

Cole was from Wolffton, a nearby village and Wes was local. The two had met on a road work project and been friends ever since. Both were extremely good-looking, tall and clean-shaven, well-built and plainly dressed. Wes had a wonderful smile that he beamed at Connie. Cole made small talk while I listened, impressed that such a handsome man would turn his attention to me.

We spent the rest of that afternoon and evening together until it was time for Pa to pick us up at the fair entrance. Wes asked Connie for her address and said they would both come by if we didn't mind. And Connie, of course, didn't mind at all. Neither did I, but I just looked at Cole and left it up to Connie to make arrangements.

I didn't for a moment believe that Cole would come calling.

PART TWO

Transitions and struggles

The following weekend, Cole and Wes came to the house together. Wes had bought a new automobile and asked if we would like to go for a spin. I introduced both Cole and Wes to Ma and Pa...Connie was too busy oohing and aahing over the car. Ma nodded coolly to both, as she often did among strangers, and said nothing. Pa watched both men from the moment they arrived and I saw him give a slight nod and smile toward Wes, whose own wide smile was hard to resist. Pa had already looked Cole up and down and his eyes were direct when he extended his hand. They shook hands and Pa nodded, but neither man smiled. When Cole turned, I thought his face was a little flushed.

"Come on," Connie called. She was in the car already, impatient to be off.

That was the beginning. We took many automobile rides, as long as weather allowed, visited every fair in three counties, and got to know each others' families.

Wes worked in his family's construction business, hauling lumber, sand, and gravel. Cole had no steady job but also worked construction, sometimes alongside Wes. Cole's family were business owners who had lost their profitable general store in a fire.

"Someone set it alight," said Cole. "It happened over the July 4th holiday, and officers said it was a fire cracker gone astray. That's not what happened, though. Someone set it, probably because Father wouldn't extend credit or something like that."

Cole had hoped to share the business with his father later but now that dream was gone. The wonderful brick home where he was born had been sold, just to pay bills and get by. There had been no insurance on the store.

"But anyway," Cole had added, his voice rising a little, "Father wanted my brother, Perry, to help with the store. Perry was more suited to mercantile, Father said, more reliable, better with people. What he meant was that I wouldn't let people walk all over me, like Perry. He's such a weak sister, always has been." He paused. "Come to think of it, a family partnership probably wouldn't have worked out, anyhow."

Everywhere we went, Cole turned feminine heads. Women would look at him and smile, flounce their skirts or pat their hair. He would smile back and sometimes look over his shoulder to see if the woman was looking back. More than one woman acted as if she knew him but when I asked Cole about it, he just laughed and said it was my imagination. Nonetheless, it was obvious he liked admiration, whether from friend or stranger.

I had secured a teaching contract just weeks after my state certification came through. My school was like schools sprinkled across the state, a one-room affair with a wood stove, outside privy, and a wide span of grades. That first year I had seventeen students, ages six to sixteen. Several of the students were taller than me, and I was careful not to stand beside them. We had been told at County Normal to avoid letting students see that teacher wasn't the tallest in the room. Tall suggested authority, I suppose, and short meant vulnerable. So with my five-foot frame, not standing among taller farm boys proved to be a challenge.

Wes taught me how to drive his car, not a complicated task, and I bought a car to drive to school. I also made arrangements with a family near the school to stay there during bad weather. Cole liked my little 1924 Ford coupe and drove it when we were together. It wasn't right, he said, for a woman to be driving when she was with a man.

Meanwhile, Connie quit high school mid-term. She just got tired of it, she said, but I suspected there was more to it than that. She wasn't sixteen yet, and should have been in school, but who's to make her? Not Ma or Pa. Ma said it was her choice to stay home and Pa said he hoped she would be a help to Ma now that she was home all day.

Connie wasn't at home all day. Whenever Wes was available, whether it was evening, weekends, a day rained-off the job, or days between jobs, Connie was with him. She told me that summer that she and Wes were getting married.

"You're too young," I told her flatly. "You don't know anything about men or marriage or responsibility. You've been babied and taken care of your whole life."

"Oh, pshaw," Connie replied, not the least put off. "There's nothing to knowing about men. All you have to do is say how strong and handsome they are and give them a little loving once in a while."

"Connie!" I couldn't believe these words were coming from my baby sister's mouth.

"Come on, Amy, don't pretend you don't know what I'm talking about. What's so secret about this love business, anyway? There's not much to it, really. I don't know why Wes likes it so much. He's real nice to me when he wants it." Connie laughed, that tinkling bell laugh.

I needed to end this conversation. So I said, "Just remember where babies come from, Connie. Or take Ma's words to heart.

Remember when she said that the way to prevent babies is to sleep with your feet in a crock?"

"So who's sleeping? Besides, we're getting married in October," Connie said, her tone turned sullen. "I'm not staying on the farm my whole life and you should think about that, too. You're almost nineteen, after all. Maybe you can snag Cole, if you play it right. It might do you some good to try giving a little."

Cole had already said more or less the same thing.

"We've been seeing each other for months now," he said. "You know I like girls and that girls like me. I could have my pick of any girl in the county, and I think you know that. I've chosen you and see you the most. But that's not enough. We need to do what boys and girls do when they care. You do care about me, don't you?"

Being with Cole was exciting. He was not afraid of anything; not afraid of racing cars or horses or any number of stunts that entertained or irritated. He even got in the ring with a boxer at one of the fairs and won a little trophy for me. Truth to tell, I was more afraid of getting pregnant than of losing my virginity. I had to answer Cole's question, or thought I did, so I nodded and said "yes" in a voice not much more than a whisper. It seemed enough to mollify Cole, at least for awhile.

When Wes and Connie were married later that year, Cole and I were at their sides. This was not a big wedding, just a justice-of-the-peace thing, but Connie looked very pretty and I caught the bouquet at the reception.

That may have been the impetus for Cole's proposal. I told Ma and Pa after Cole left that evening. Ma said nothing at first, only looked at me in the way she did when picking words carefully.

"What about your teaching, Amy? You have the means to an independent life. Shall you give it up so easily?"

"I'm not giving it up, Ma. My contract's still in, and I can work and be married. Actually, we need the money, what with Cole not working."

"What with Cole not working," Pa echoed. "Does he have plans for work, for supporting you? Never mind. Please sit down, Amy."

We all sat and Pa continued. "Amy, it's not for me to say who you marry, and I'm not. But this Cole, he's not like us. He's a high roller with no money and little credit. I have asked around a bit and Cole is known across two counties as a brawler with a mean temper. He's a charmer when he wants and some say he's a woman chaser who trades on his looks. I don't think he is the one for you, Amy. There's bound to be a solid, kind, supportive husband for you out there someplace. Someone whose family has land, a husband worth waiting for."

I saw Ma nod in agreement, and said nothing. I wasn't going to argue with my folks over this. But for once, I didn't say, "Yes, Pa."

Cole and I were married four months later. We moved in with his parents on their farm near Wolffton.

Chapter Two

The Morgan farm was not the kind of farm I was used to. Farm implements stood outside, rusting in the weather. Fields lay fallow and the barns housed only a few scruffy animals. Even with snow on the ground, chickens ran loose, scratching for sustenance wherever they could find it. Inside the house, rooms were dark and wallpaper dingy. Pa and Cole moved Mrs. Smithson's piano into the parlor, where its polished wood gleamed like a jewel against the faded walls. There was a basement with a coal furnace, if you had any coal. Otherwise, wood provided what heat there was, the central furnace supplemented by the wood-burning kitchen range. Water was pumped by hand from a well not far from the back door. A somewhat dilapidated privy stood beyond, far enough away to deter visits on winter nights. At least there was electricity for lights.

Father Morgan was nothing like Pa. Every morning Pa was up early, tending to his animals and the fields. Father Morgan worked slower, later, and relied on Mother Morgan and other family members for much of the work. That meant us. Not just us, as it turned out, because Cole's brother, Perry, and his new wife, Mildred, soon moved in as well. So there were seven of us, including Cole's ten-year-old sister, Alice.

Thank goodness the house was large. The upstairs was soon divided by nailing up temporary partitions, so that each family had a private area of two or three rooms, and Alice had her own bedroom.

Downstairs, though, there was only one kitchen and one dining room so we all ate together. "Together" may not be the appropriate word. Mealtimes were contentious and the animosity between Cole and Perry was never entirely below the surface. Father Morgan might say, "Let's all eat in peace," or even, "Judas priest, Cole, will you let it be for now?" and sometimes Mother Morgan would murmur something. It was Mildred who never shut up. Maybe she thought she could neutralize Cole's attacks on Perry, or even change Cole's behavior. She constantly defended Perry's words, actions, character, appearance--it just went on and on. Perry rarely defended himself, and I was never sure whether this behavior signified confidence or inferiority. Either way, I appreciated his silence and contributed my own.

Mildred's maiden name was Berkshire, same as a well-known breed of pigs, and when her needling words went too far for Cole, he would simply lean across the table into her face and say, in a falsetto voice, "oink, oink, oink." This trick unfailingly reduced Mildred to tears and she would race away from the table, followed by Perry. This left us with a few moments of blissful silence, unless, that is, Father Morgan continued with a stream of his own criticisms aimed at Cole.

I was glad to have work that took me away from this unsettling place. The roads were still winter rough, and I suggested to Cole that it made more sense for me to stay near the school during these months. He objected at first, saying the roads weren't impassable and that he wanted me home nights. What changed his mind was the idea that he could keep the car all week if he drove me to school Sundays and picked me up Friday.

My paycheck was the only steady income that year at the Morgan farm. As spring drew closer, Father Morgan suggested I buy a pair of young pigs that could be raised for profit. I don't recall now whether they were Berkshires. This was the first of many "investments" I made in the Morgan farm.

I wondered what Cole did all week while I was at school. Sometimes he would tell me as we drove back to the farm. I quickly learned that the events of his week generally determined the mood of the weekend. Usually he had some money-making story to tell—a day's trucking, a win at the pool hall, some find alongside the road that he turned into cash. These plus stories were intermingled with minuses...Perry got a trucking job he should have had, some bigwig in town snubbed him, he was cheated out of a win at the card room.

Then there was the day he gave me the garter. Cole's mood was high that day and he greeted me with a warm hug and kiss. I tucked my valise into the car and as soon as our trip started, details of Cole's week began to pour out—he had taxied one of the councilmen to the city and was paid well, including two meals. He had bought his mother a pair of shoes—hers were no longer worth fixing. The piglets were thriving and "get this," Cole said, with a slap to the steering wheel, "feeding them is Perry's job." Then he reached in his pocket, withdrew this satin circlet and handed it to me.

"A trophy," he said, laughing. "That girl at the bar just dared me and Mr. Councilman egged me on."

I was stunned. "Are you saying a woman was wearing this garter and you took it from her?"

"Well, yeah. Otherwise, what's the fun?"

I was still holding the thing, looking at it, not really looking at it.

"But Cole, you're my husband, you're pledged to me. This just isn't right."

I could sense his mood change. "Sure, I'm your husband. That doesn't mean you own me. And this—this elastic—it doesn't mean anything. I didn't even know the girl."

When we reached the farm, I went to our rooms upstairs. Cole didn't follow and I sat on the bed, thinking. No tears flowed, no cries or sobs escaped. Cole thought this betrayal was nothing.

I still held the garter in my hand, feeling the tube elastic encased beneath red satin ribbon and lace. The cover had been sewn on by hand, not very skillfully, either. I tried to imagine what kind of tart would make such a thing, and why? I didn't like the thoughts that came and I tossed the thing on the bed.

Pa had been right about Cole. I should just leave now, go back home to Pa and Ma, put this bad dream behind me. It would be hard to face Pa, to admit he was right. Ma would just say it was my choice to go or stay. Connie would be unsympathetic and probably say it was my fault, what with her storybook romance continuing.

I got the scissors from my sewing basket. It took only a few seconds to snip the loose stitching that held the ribbon in place. I snipped the ribbon and lace into tiny bits and stuffed them in my pocket. I would get rid of them later, in the trash bucket at school.

The elastic underneath was just like the circlets I used to roll my own hose. Stripped of its tawdry dressing, the garter was respectable again, nearly new, clean and un-frayed. I put it with my hosiery, against the time when one of my own might break. Waste not, want not. I brushed my hair and went downstairs to supper.

Chapter Three

That summer Father Morgan, Cole, and Perry focused their attention on the farm. Alfalfa, timothy, and corn flourished in the fields, a team of horses was acquired, the pigs grew fat, and the cattle looked more sleek. It seemed that Father Morgan, Perry, and Cole could work together after all, and everyone's mood lightened as the season wore on. Mother Morgan, Mildred, Alice, and I planted a garden and tended it from seed to harvest. A nice assortment of canned vegetables lined basement shelves by summer's end.

One of the cows calved, an immaculate conception I supposed, until Cole said he had smuggled the animal into the neighbor's field in timely fashion. "Wasn't nearly as easy getting her out of there as it was letting her in," Cole said. "That bull just didn't want me in his territory." Cole laughed, remembering the adventure, and perhaps at the horrified expression on my face. He gave me a hug and tickled me until I laughed too.

Father Morgan, instead of just commenting about the tumble-down porch, repaired it. Using stones picked from the fields, he replaced decaying wood supports with a foundation and wall. Stones were nicely fitted and cemented into place along the entire length. Mother Morgan told me that her husband was an experienced stone worker. "He can build things," she said, "houses and such. He has a real way with stones and brick. Sometimes he talks about giving up farming and spending all his time building."

Meanwhile, Father Morgan rediscovered a book given to him a few years earlier. The book came from a former University of Michigan student who remembered when Father and Mother Morgan operated a boarding house in Ann Arbor during the author's deanship at the university. Father Morgan gave the book to Cole, and Cole couldn't put it down. The book was Primitive Man in Michigan by W.B. Hinsdale. The work was a study of the state's Indian peoples, their culture, settlements, and burial mounds. There were sketches and photos of Indian-made tools and other artifacts, descriptions of the materials in each and the various techniques used to create them. Burial mounds were said to be the primary source for what relics remained. Hinsdale—whose goal was to preserve the history and remnants of Michigan's Indian culture—had unknowingly provided Cole with a how-to book for locating, identifying, and looting a people's heritage.

Cole pointed out that Hinsdale's map identified no Indian burial mounds in our county. This meant to Cole that there were unknown treasures to be found, riches to be discovered. That year we toured the county every weekend, looking for hills that might be "mounds." That we didn't find any didn't mean to Cole that there weren't any. It only meant that we hadn't looked in the right place.

We also drove to county fairs, enjoying the rides and sideshows as if we were without a care in the world. I can still see Cole flexing his muscles and swinging that big mallet back and forth at the "Test Your Strength" machine. This was a contraption that looked like a tall inverted thermometer. The idea was to strike a small pad at the bottom with a large wooden mallet, driving a ball upwards to ring the bell at the top. "Degrees" marked the progress of the ball upward, beginning with "weakling" near the bottom and "champion" at the top. Cole would usually take off his jacket or shirt and hand it to me with a flourish before taking the mallet. His posing and practice swings generally drew a small crowd and cheers when he finally struck the base pad and the bell clanged. Sometimes bets were made on how many consecutive times he could ring the bell. It wasn't beyond Cole to begin with a light blow or two to drive up the betting. This little show was highly entertaining to me, and I liked being identified, to all who cared to look at the shirt I was holding, as "his girl." Cole called the money from the bets "found money," which meant we could spend it on anything. That's what we did.

My contract was renewed at the school and, toward the end of summer, Cole suggested I buy a new car. My little Ford was showing some wear so I agreed. That's how it happened that I bought a snazzy little maroon Chrysler with a rumble seat, financed on the basis of my teaching contract.

It had been an optimistic summer. Everyone worked hard on the farm, and there were few disagreements. We had food put by for the winter, and the barn was full of hay for the horses and cattle. Not to say that everything was perfect…while Cole and I were having fun at the fairs, Father Morgan sold the two pigs I bought and pocketed the money.

On a Friday, a few weeks after school opened, Cole was late picking me up. I waited until six o'clock and telephoned Father Morgan's nearest neighbors. I asked if they would check on Cole's whereabouts for me, explaining my predicament. The neighbors knew the Morgans had no telephone and were glad to oblige. When they called me back an hour later, I learned that Cole had taken off for Kentucky with a friend and my Chrysler. I was stuck at school until the next week.

Chapter Four

Of course Cole had an explanation for taking off for Kentucky and leaving me stranded. He said it was about a job and money, high priority issues. Father Morgan's brother had written to say that he was in the middle of a building project in Lexington. The work included land clearance, basements, chimneys, and sidewalks. It was a big undertaking and would Father Morgan and his boys like to make a few bucks? Cole wanted to see what this offer was all about, his friend Harper was at loose ends, and I was not available. He said I should be pleased that he was looking into money-making opportunities. I was pleased, but I resented the thought that I was at the bottom on his priority list. Rather than make matters worse by pursuing that thought, I let it go.

It was true that money was an everyday issue. In spite of extra efforts on crops and animals, the farm mortgage was getting further behind. Father Morgan asked Cole and Perry to help make payments, saying that money we paid would buy a piece of the farm. Father Morgan said it was a way for Cole and Perry to get started with small acreage and a place to build. Finally we would own our own land and build our own place. The prospect was exciting, and I agreed, making payments to Father Morgan every month.

Father and Mother Morgan took Alice and went to Kentucky. Perry and Mildred joined them, leaving Cole and me alone on the farm. We took out the partition between our upstairs rooms and his parents' rooms and reveled in the extra space. We slept in their feather bed and enjoyed dinners by ourselves. Cole's mood was high during those hours spent together, and I was reminded why I had loved him to begin with, and still did. I felt so much more alive when he was with me.

Some evenings I played piano, remembering those wonderful evenings when Mrs. Smithson had played for us. I played pieces I knew, that she had taught me. Other times I practiced pieces for school plays and events. I thought Cole would find the music as pleasing as I did, and I didn't understand his reaction. He said I was ignoring him, that the songs weren't musical, that the whole exercise was unnecessary. His complaint was a red flag I should have seen. Instead, I ignored Cole's comments and continued playing.

And so it was that Cole decided to turn my beloved piano into a makeshift cabinet to hold some unnamed things we didn't own. I came home to find the piano's inner workings piled in crates, its wonderful polished wood butchered into rectangles and scrap. The cupboard Cole assembled from these pieces was a monstrosity.

It was just too much. I screamed and collapsed in tears and sobs. I cried for most of that weekend, mourning the loss of my most valued possession, this irreplaceable treasure.

"Quit bawling," is what Cole said. "The piano was useless, and we don't need useless trash. The cabinet is useful."

There was nothing to do except tell Pa and Ma. They rarely came to the Morgan farm, might not have known about the loss of my piano for months, but I had to tell someone. Ma patted my hand and sympathized. Pa told me to think about what was important and to fit my decisions to that.

I drove back to the farm to think. If I left Cole, he would be furious. If I divorced him, it would be worse. Further, I would probably lose my teaching position...divorced women were not generally seen as desirable tutors for impressionable children.

As it turned out, the decision was made for me. I was pregnant. Now there was no way I could leave Cole, return home, or even continue teaching for very long. I told myself that things would change for the better when we had a baby.

Cole seemed pleased. He said a son would be nice, the Morgans always had sons. I just knew that our life would be different when that son was born.

Father and Mother Morgan returned briefly from Kentucky to say we would have to find another place to live. The bank was foreclosing the farm. Perry had already rented a farm for himself and Mildred and he would take the animals. I asked about all those payments I had made toward land. Father Morgan turned away in disgust and Mother Morgan chided me, "You got to live there, didn't you?"

Before the bank people showed up to lock the doors, Father Morgan planned to auction everything they couldn't take back to Kentucky.

Cole found us a little house a mile west of Wolffton and we moved our few belongings there. No one had taken the canned jars of vegetables and fruits from the prior summer so I took them all. At least we would have some food in our pantry. We brought our clothes and little else, mostly because we had little else.

Auction day was sunny and clear, a good omen for attracting buyers. A medium-sized crowd gathered, many of them neighbors and local farmers. But there were others, too, men in city hats and shiny shoes unfit for walking through barns and fields. The farm implements and equipment sold first, and then the furnishings from the house. Mother Morgan's sideboard was gone in a minute, for hardly half its true value. Her table and chairs, cooking pots and washtub, all slipped away into buyers' hands. Then I noticed it. The little cabinet that had once been my prized piano. It was up for bids. Someone bid fifty cents. Seventy-five. Sold. I walked to where the buyer stood, looking at his purchase.

"Poor workmanship," he was saying, "but the wood is good. The wood is real good. It'll be a useful cupboard for May's kitchen."

Mother Morgan was nowhere in sight, and I wished I had been as smart. All these vultures picking over the scraps of hard times, buying up hard-won and cherished belongings for pennies. I walked away then and waited in the barn until Cole was ready to leave.

The house we rented was actually a former schoolhouse, abandoned when the larger school had been built in town. The school had two rooms, otherwise it was typical…wood stove, outside privy. We had a kerosene stove for cooking, and I set up a makeshift kitchen in the smaller room. The land around the building was tall with grass and weeds and so it remained. Home beautification was the least of our worries.

This small house had its advantages. Communal dinners would be a thing of the past. For the first time, Cole and I weren't living under his parents' roof. Not inclined toward romanticizing, I nonetheless dubbed the place "the cottage." Such girlish elation would be short-lived.

Within months, Father and Mother Morgan returned with Alice from Kentucky. There had been a falling out with Uncle and Father Morgan just wasn't going to take his orders any longer. Uncle would just have to find some other flunkey. Father Morgan looked for a place to rent and, in the meantime, the family slept on the floor in our meager space. Within days, thank goodness, they found a place a short mile north and moved in there.

Catherine Frances was born that autumn at the cottage. Cole was disappointed to have a daughter instead of a son and left it up to me to choose a name. I chose Catherine, for Mrs.

Smithson's daughter, who took such good care of me when I had typhoid. Frances, Cole's middle name, was meant to please both Cole and Mother Morgan.

Cole spent most of his time now at the warmly heated card room downtown, playing cards, and shooting pool for money. By whatever means, he won more often than he lost and I was grateful, even though I nearly froze in the drafty house. My income was sorely missed--by the entire clan, I thought ruefully. I nursed Catherine and kept her warmly bundled as the winter wore on. My car was repossessed and, with rent unpaid, we were ordered to move.

Cole and Catherine and I moved back in with Father and Mother Morgan who were waging their own battle against eviction. Then Father Morgan dropped a bombshell. He said we would be moving into the old farmhouse on the original Morgan homestead.

Cole's surprise was evident in his comment, "You said you sold the farm before I was born."

Father Morgan shrugged and didn't reply.

The once proud Morgan farm originally encompassed more than half of Wolffton itself. Great chunks had been sold off when the railroad came through and the rest, or most of it anyway, nibbled away one parcel at a time for village housing.

Whoever had been living in the house had moved out, escaped, leaving the house for us. This development, great blessing that it was, seems surreal even now, considering the losses, foreclosures, and hard times of the past several years. Had Father Morgan always owned this place? Had he got it back through foreclosure or eviction? We were not to know and Mother Morgan said her husband had done nothing wrong. The Morgans made house deals among themselves all the time, she said, and if Father Morgan chose to keep those dealings to himself, that was his privilege. There was no sense asking more.

The house had been built just after the Civil War on a small hill, the property's highest point, a hint, perhaps of the glory expected by the newly arrived Morgans. The two-story house faced west, toward and over the village, with a parlor and dining room across the front. A good-sized kitchen and small pantry lay behind. There was one small bedroom downstairs off the parlor and two larger bedrooms upstairs. Cooking and heating fuel was stored in a lean-to shed behind the kitchen. There was no electricity or plumbing and water came from an outside pump.

The parlor exited onto a narrow covered porch that ran nearly the entire width of the house. This porch, sheltered by nearby trees, proved to be a fine spot for summer sun and breezes. There was a cellar, too, useful for storage, washing clothes in inclement weather, and as emergency shelter from passing cyclones.

As an aside to this bucolic description, let me add that one of Father Morgan's first acts was to nail up a partition between the parlor and dining room. It was a thin wood barrier, more a screen than a wall, with an open space at the top. Cole, Catherine, and I were allotted the space with the parlor, bedroom, and front door. The remaining space belonged to Father and Mother Morgan and Alice.

Mother Morgan confided that it wasn't her choice to divide the house this way. She said they just wanted a little peace, a little space to themselves. She hoped that avoiding conflicts between Cole and his father would work to my advantage too. "Just tap on the wall if you need anything," she said, "Or if you'd like me to take Catherine for a while."

A chimney was hastily installed at the end of the living room and our wood-burning stove set in place. Once again, we found ourselves living with Father and Mother Morgan, not together, but separately.

I pumped our water outside and Mother Morgan did the same. We took our turns walking the distance to the privy. We bathed in our own rooms, using basins or galvanized tubs and poured our waste water outside. We slung it from the porch or dumped wash water on the front edge of the lawn. There was something satisfying in watching that used water flow lazily down the hillside and on toward town.

Chapter Five

Summers at the Morgan farmstead were pleasant enough. Mother Morgan and I tended the garden and chickens and walked the lane from barn to pasture. There was one cow and one horse, which Father Morgan tended. He seemed content here and, of an evening, I often heard him singing while he milked Bessie. There were neither farm tools requiring horsepower, nor buggies and carts to be drawn, so owning a horse seemed wasteful. Star was a saddle horse, ridden regularly by Alice and sometimes by Cole and Father Morgan. It occurred to me that Star was like my piano: both were beautiful and both were "useless," in a utilitarian sense. I watched Star grazing the field behind the barn, her chestnut hindquarters gleaming under the sun like well-polished wood. Shame on me that I was wondering how Cole would feel if Star were turned into a more practical product, such as soap or glue. Yes, I kept that thought to myself, hiding it among the other mean thoughts that were accumulating day by day in my heart.

The bright spot in my life was Catherine. She went with me everywhere…the chicken coop, garden, on my walks downtown. Mother Morgan tended her too, coddling her first grandchild as first-time grandmothers do.

Cole was home less and less as he looked for dollars at the pool hall, trucked vegetables to the city, scraped for whatever work could be found. Interest in the stone porch at the foreclosed farm had led to offers of other stonework, "manna from heaven" was the way Mother Morgan put it. Cole often helped his father with these projects and they built chimneys, fireplaces, entrance pillars, and retaining walls as chance supplied.

One afternoon a man I'd not seen before knocked on the parlor door. He was holding a large roundish stone with a dish-like hollow on one side and looking for Cole. Cole was in the barn that day, grooming Star, and so I directed the visitor to the barn and watched from the porch as Cole came outside and the two men talked. The visitor began shouting. I could hear the sound but not the words…he was waving his arms menacingly, finally flinging the stone to the ground. As he turned to leave, I heard him say, "…by tomorrow."

Cole was visibly shaken by the encounter. He said he had to come up with five dollars by the next day.

It turned out that Cole and Father Morgan had found this stone somewhere on the farm. Cole said it resembled a picture of an Indian mortar he had seen in Hinsdale's book so they decided to enhance that resemblance by pounding and pecking the rock. The hollowed side was enlarged and deepened and then the whole thing soaked in grit and used motor oil to restore color. The "relic" sold for five dollars, which Cole had duly spent. On what, I had no idea.

Unfortunately, the buyer decided the stone was dirty and needed cleaning. Scrubbing off the oil exposed the lighter color of the "enhanced" area and the buyer was livid. If Cole didn't come up with the money by tomorrow, he would go to the sheriff.

Cole went looking for his father and stayed out until late that night. No sheriff came to the door so he must have found the money somewhere. This was another sleeping dog I let lie.

Every summer, when the county fairs came around, Cole got a boy's itchy feet. Those feet yearned to walk the crowded midways and tread the makeshift aisles in the sideshow tents. The "Test Your Strength" machine drew him like a magnet, along with other games of strength or skill.

"Let's go to the fair," he said one evening. "This is the biggest night of the week. It will be fun, you can ride the Ferris wheel."

"Catherine's already asleep," I said.

"No, I don't mean Catherine. Just us two, like it used to be. Mother can keep an eye on her from the other rooms."

I didn't like the idea of leaving Catherine like that. The day's tasks had been wearing besides, and I was tired.

"Why don't you just go, Cole? It's already late, and I'll be up early with Catherine. My energy's about spent, anyway."

That was all the encouragement Cole needed. In minutes I heard his car spin down the drive and into the night. With luck, I could gain a few hours sleep before he returned.

Cole woke me up after midnight. I was dozing on the parlor davenport when he shook me awake.

"Amy, Amy," he said, his eyes wild. "I think I killed a man."

"How? What happened, Cole? Tell me." I was wide awake now.

"I won this canary in a cage. I carried it around for a while, then went to take it to the field where the car was parked." His voice was shaking, and the hand I held was trembling.

"All at once this guy jumped me. He must've been drunk, 'cause he was way undersized to take me on, but he takes this swing at me and says, 'Gimmee that tweeter.' I swung back without thinking, caught him hard side the head and he went down face first. I set the cage down and rolled the guy over. He seemed okay, just out.

"Well, next thing, I went back to the midway, I don't know why. Just to catch my breath, maybe get help. The canary cage was still in the field and I just walked around for a while, about an hour, didn't tell anybody, and then decided to come home. Well, the guy was still lying there, just like I left him. He looked dead. Somebody had taken the bird."

I put my arms around him, hoping to ease his trembling. Finally I asked, "Should we go to the sheriff?"

"No, no, I thought of that. It's too late for that, now. We'll just wait. I'll get a paper tomorrow, see what it says."

Now that Cole was calmer, he moved to find a cup and retrieve the fifth he kept stashed in the dresser drawer. The generous pour he splashed into the cup was gone in two swallows.

We watched the newspapers, searching for items that might provide clues. There were none, not even in the obituaries.

"I told you he was drunk," Cole said, after a week or so. "I just cold-cocked a drunk and helped him sleep it off. Nothing wrong with that."

The winter of 1932 stands out in memory for its heavy snow and incessant icy winds. Our stacks of stove wood on the porch were buried under deep snow. Every day I dug out armloads of wood for the stove, and every day whirling winds replaced what snow I had scraped away. In the stove, wet logs sizzled and flames sometimes fizzled under the melt. At least our fuel wasn't in the barn. Cole had stacked the lengths on the porch, closer, he said, so I didn't have to walk so far.

Catherine spent most of that winter on the parlor davenport. The floors were too cold for her little legs, and I worried that she would get sick. Some days winds pushed under the door with force enough to raise the carpet. I spoke to Cole about it.

"It's what we have," he told me. "Things will get better, but we've got to get through this winter. I've got some ideas for big money this summer. You'll see."

"But Catherine..."

"No buts, Amy," Cole interrupted. "You always want more." He was shouting now. "More, more, more. Nothing is ever enough for Sam and Addy's daughter."

Catherine began to cry. All at once her cries became wheezing, and she gasped for breath. She was crying and wheezing and gasping for breath while Cole was ranting on about my greed and Mother Morgan was wading through the snow from the back door to the front door, into the parlor and straight on to her grandchild.

Catherine had had her first asthma attack.

Chapter Six

Dr. Mercer came to the house and prescribed medicine for Catherine. He said she might be allergic and we should watch for things that might trigger attacks. We had the medicine compounded at the drug store downtown and waited.. There was nothing else to do, except keep Catherine away from Cole's outbursts. To my mind, they were the likely cause of her distress.

As soon as the weather cleared, Cole began digging a shallow pit near the barn, a fire pit, he said, for his new project. He brought various pieces of equipment home and set them up inside the barn. I asked him what he was doing and his response was, "Just never mind, you'll see."

So one afternoon when Cole was gone, Catherine and I went to see. We saw a machine that looked like a cement mixer and an assortment of grinding wheels, more than anyone needed to keep household implements sharpened. There was a small gasoline engine rigged with belts to drive the wheels and mixer. Cole had hammered together a large work bench from scrap wood…it was arrayed with chisels and drilling tools, large and small hammers, alongside other unfamiliar pointed and sharp hand tools. Maybe I didn't want to know what Cole was planning.

The fire pit burned for days on end that summer, and I could hear the mechanical roll of the cement mixer as it tumbled and turned. It became clear that no cement was being mixed…no sidewalks or other evidence came to be. I stayed away from the barn all that season, except to cross into the lane where Mother Morgan, Catherine, and I walked.

I was pregnant again and not too pleased at the prospect of bringing another baby into our two-room compartment. Something had to happen, and I needed to figure out a plan of action. One thing I had learned during my years with Cole was that he acted more quickly if there was a benefit for him. Any argument for new living quarters needed to be based on what he needed, not on what I wanted for me, Catherine, or the new baby.

It didn't make it easier that Cole had just created the barn workshop. One afternoon he came in from the barn with a rectangular smooth stone in his hand. The long edges and one end were blunted and curved, with the remaining side narrowed to a sharp edge. I looked at the stone in his extended hand. He was smiling, pleased with himself. "Skinning stone," he said. "As good as any celt Hinsdale pictured in his Indian book. Two days in the tumbler and two more in the pit and it looks pretty old. Can't wash this baby clean."

Now I really knew what Cole was "building" in the barn. Suspecting is one thing, knowing is another, and I didn't like it much.

"What will you do with it?" I knew the answer, but dreaded it.

"Sell it, Amy. Sell it. There's a big market for these things, and I can tap into it. Lots of ways. For starters, I have about a pail full of stones I picked up from that mound I spotted south of here. They're real enough and an occasional 'ringer' isn't going to be noticed. This could be big time, Amy. There'll be more money for all of us."

That, at least, was welcome news. Maybe the extra money would help us find a new place. Soon after that, an opportunity came as I was walking downtown. A "for rent" sign was displayed in the window of a somewhat rundown house less than two blocks from the Morgan farmstead. I knocked on the door.

An older woman came to the door, invited me in, and told me her story. She was moving in with a daughter, could no longer afford the house or keep it up. She showed me the downstairs, its one bedroom, open stairway and sunny living room with west-facing window. The kitchen and dining room were small, with a sink and pump. She said there were two bedrooms up and a cellar if I wanted to see the rest of the house.

"Not today," I said, "But I do like it. How much rent are you asking?" She told me, and I said I would let her know after talking to my husband.

"I'll need a few days," she said, her voice quavering.

"Of course," I told her, "We have a few days."

I was jubilant. This house stood in clear view from the farmstead—downhill, of course—on land that once was a part of the Greater Morgan farm. The location was close to Cole's barn workshop and the back shed could provide more work space. There was room for a garden, and room for two children or more. How to sell the idea to Cole? He had to think it was his idea.

It took a few days. I mentioned the house, mentioned it again. I suggested that Cole needed more room, a place to call his own, and space distanced from his parents. He might notice it on his way downtown if he drove that block. It was a wonderful moment when he said, "I checked into that house for rent and we can move in the first of the month." Music to my ears, as Ma might say.

When Sarah was born a few months later, four-year-old Catherine had her own room upstairs and the baby slept in a basket beside our bed. The house was no castle, but it was no colder than the Morgan farmstead in winter and roomier all year round. Having my own kitchen, cook stove, and electricity seemed almost luxurious. When Pa found and bought a kitchen cupboard with a built-in flour bin, I was delighted. Cole frowned and told Pa he could provide whatever was needed and Pa just smiled and agreed, saying that "this little cupboard" wasn't really very much anyway, and he had picked it up for practically nothing. And he extended his hand to Cole, with a "Good to see you," and said good-bye. Cole was mollified. And Pa did it with just a few words and a smile. Not so simple for me.

The devastating news some months later was that the house was to be sold. The owner-landlady needed to cash out her holdings. The idea of moving again was just too much. Cole just shrugged and said we'd likely have to move. I decided to talk to Mother Morgan.

"Alice has some money now," Mother Morgan said. "Now that she's teaching school and still living at home, there's money to spare. Why not ask her if she'll help out?"

Alice? Cole's baby sister. I spoke to Cole about it and he seemed as surprised as I was that she might be able to help. But would she? Why should she?

And in 1935, who would have believed that we would be rescued by a fledgling teacher who, it turned out, had an eye for thrift and a head for money. She bought the house. Cole and I signed a land contract and became land owners for the first time in our lives. Forever after I remained grateful to Alice, and as the years passed, we became close, as close or closer than I was to Connie, my blood sister.

Now that the place was ours, Cole took a new interest in its upkeep and appearance. He replaced the sagging kitchen ceiling, refitted and puttied loose windows and sealed seams against the weather. He brought in loads of gravel for the muddy driveway and filled the smaller shed with fuel for the stoves. He even built a child-size easel for Catherine, so impressed was he with her drawings and designs.

Cole moved his barn workshop into the shed out back. The fire pit was replaced by a metal drum with one side open and charcoal piled inside. Cole set this drum in hollowed out ground behind the shop. "Away from neighbors' prying eyes," he said. A wood barrel tumbler replaced the cement mixer and tumbled, untended, for hours on end now that we had a place with electricity. The shop was producing more pieces.

The road building projects Cole worked on were seldom nearby and he often stayed on the job all week, coming home on weekends. Whenever he traveled to a new area—Kalamazoo, Bad Axe, St. Johns—he would take a few "relics" with him.

"I'll just show these to guys in the bars," he told me. "We end up in bars most nights, and maybe I can sell one or two. And it's good to keep these deals away from home. Once our work is done and we leave, no one knows where we went or who we are. Less chance of buyers getting together." And he laughed.

I liked having my own place and, more than that, was grateful that the money was there to pay Alice. She came by every month, regular as clockwork, to pick up her payment.

I had always looked at Alice as a mere girl, a child, Cole's quiet baby sister. That image was gone. She had become a confident young woman, a country school teacher like me. Hers was a calm, smiling presence, and I looked forward to her visits. She was always glad to see me, too, and, like Mother Morgan, adored Catherine.

Alice spent hours with her, going on walks, playing games, reading stories, and singing. This was a great break for me. Need I say that I appreciated Alice more than ever?

Chapter Seven

In the winter of 1936 I was pregnant again. Sarah was not quite two and I worried that Cole might take this news badly, but he only shrugged and commented that "maybe it will be a boy this time." Unlike the others, this was not a comfortable pregnancy. I felt vaguely unwell, lacking the sense of well-being I'd experienced with Catherine and Sarah. My fatigue just grew as the winter wore on and I barely had the energy to take care of the girls, let alone for housework and cooking. I wished Cole would help more with Catherine and Sarah, but hints fell on deaf ears, and I dared not ask directly.

Cole was not working, what with road construction at a standstill until spring. He fell into his old pattern at the pool hall and card room but seemed to have lost his enthusiasm for the games. He seemed restless and his stories of winning and putting-one-over on one sucker or another lacked zest. Some days, when the weather wasn't too frigid, Cole worked his stones in the unheated workshop. Then, in March, he was laid low by a sore throat that Dr. Mercer said was strep. Cole was ordered to bed, and I was given detailed instructions on preparing his needed liquid diet. I was already exhausted and this was the last straw. I went over to the neighbor's and telephoned Ma.

Ma came over that day. She cooked, she cleaned, she changed the sheets on Cole's bed with him in it. Ma whirled around the house talking, taking charge. She reminded me how tired I looked and that I was seven months pregnant. Cole complained, but Ma ignored his demands and fed him more broth. I took a nap for the first time in memory. Cole got better.

It was so good having Ma in the house. Same old Ma, whirlwind on heels, working and talking and taking care of others. I was reminded of how much I loved her and told her so when she left. She brushed the words away, but I saw her little smile and could tell she was pleased. We didn't very often turn love into words in our family.

I was making bread the following week when someone knocked. I wiped the flour from my hands the best I could and opened the door.

"Are you Amelia Morgan?" A man I had never seen asked the question. He looked glum.

"Yes, I'm Amy. Is something wrong?"

"Well, yes, ma'am," he said, "First, let me say that I'm a neighbor of Sam Whitlock. He sent me here, you don't have a telephone, he said. He wanted me to tell you that your Ma died this morning."

I shut the door, shut out the news. Through the window I could see the man turn and walk away. Ma, dead. No, that couldn't be. She had been here just days before. I left the girls playing in the living room with an admonition to Catherine to take care of Sarah and walked across the street to the neighbor with the telephone. I called Pa.

"Yes, Amy, it's true," Pa said. "She came down sick a few days ago and we called the doctor yesterday. He said it was strep. She had no resistance to it."

"I'll figure out how to get there," I told Pa. "I'll be there as soon as I can."

I called the pool hall and asked for Cole. When I hung up the telephone receiver, I could see it was smeared with flour so I took it down and wiped it on my apron. Then I went home and kneaded and formed the bread dough that was rising in the kitchen.

Cole helped get the girls bundled up and into the car. I set the loaves on the back porch where I hoped the cold would keep them from rising too fast, grabbed my coat, and we set out.

I told Cole what Pa had said. "Strep," I said, "Same as you."

He bristled. "Are you blaming me? If blame is due, blame your Ma. She was always poking around in other people's business. If she would've stayed home, minded her own business…"

"Damn you, Cole," the words burst from my mouth, and the tears finally came. Sarah started to cry but Catherine hushed her and we continued, my weeping the only sound. Cole's face was ashen, his mouth tight, his knuckles white where he gripped the steering wheel.

I would pay for those three words. I would pay.

Chapter Eight

"I need a dress for Ma's funeral." We were home, finally, after the ride to Pa's farm. The girls were asleep, tired from the travel, tense hours and heightened activity. Family and neighbors had already begun to arrive when we got there, filling the house and spilling onto the porches. Connie was crying and crying while her husband, Wes, patted and comforted. Ivan walked around kicking the furniture. I wanted to see Pa, just to see Pa, and once that was accomplished, wanted to go home.

Cole was still simmering. "You curse me less than a few hours ago and now you want a dress. How does that work?"

"I need a dress for Ma's funeral," I repeated. "My good dress won't fit, and I can't be seen looking like this." I was wearing one of Cole's shirts to cover my large pregnancy.

"I can't afford your new dress. You'll just have to make do."

I decided to ask Mother Morgan. She seemed to know just how to get things done that needed doing. The next morning, while Cole was still asleep, I took the girls and walked up the hill to her place.

"Nothing in this house worth wearing," Mother Morgan said as she handed ginger cookies to Catherine and Sarah. "But Mildred told me Welfare has dresses. And shoes, too. I got their phone number here someplace. Get Alice to drive you there."

Cole was dead set against welfare of any kind and would have thrown a fit in the face of this advice. He had his pride, he said, and could provide everything his family needed. Sometimes I thought he would rather see us starve than eat the oranges and other food items that Welfare gave out every month at the Community Hall. Knowing Cole's strong convictions, I also knew there was just one way to handle this peaceably. I simply wouldn't tell him. Instead, I used the neighbor's phone to call Welfare Cupboard and to call Alice.

The color of the dress was Mournful Blue, or if the makers didn't call it that, they should have. The full draped skirt hiked up over my belly a bit, but otherwise was fine. It was pressed, clean, and free, and I was grateful. I took the shoes, too, thinking they would be good beyond today. They were black, with low heels and new shoelaces. Cole gave me a long look when I dressed for the service but said nothing. So I said nothing and for once, we agreed on saying nothing.

During the days that followed, I mourned Ma silently, weeping sometimes during the children's nap times. She was gone, only a few months after her fifty-ninth birthday. Childhood images of the day Ma waved goodbye and left for Traverse City State Hospital came flooding back. Every day her loss seemed brand new, sharp, and painful.

Tending the house and children helped keep my thoughts occupied. Catherine, now past seven, and Sarah, almost two, were very dissimilar children. Catherine was more active, always doing something, wanting to read, and reading, constantly looking at books I knew were beyond her. She liked to draw and paint, and studied stones and bugs and whatever else she could find outside. Catherine wished that her invisible friend, Johnny, would come down from Grandma Morgan's to visit, but he didn't, even though she called his name and waved toward the farmstead. She was lonely and sometimes talked to passing dogs and cats for company. From babyhood, Catherine was alarmed by discord and was apt to escape unpleasantness whenever possible by retreating to her upstairs room.

In contrast, Sarah didn't seem to mind commotion or quarrels. Even though she was only two, her reactions were obvious. She was interested, she was calm, she was observant. Nothing seemed to escape her baby stare as she watched and listened. Sarah rarely cried and, during Cole's occasional verbal tirades, would look first at me and then at Cole, listening to every word and following the exchanges as if at a tennis match. Sometimes all this baby scrutiny was a bit unnerving and I would pick her up and move her to another room. Sarah didn't complain about this either and could be found studying the wallpaper or the view beyond the window.

Dr. Mercer came to the house in May and delivered our son, Joseph Cole. The delivery was no more difficult than the others, Cole was delighted to have his son, and Catherine could hardly wait to take over her big sister role. Alice came and stayed for three days, tending the children and cooking.

I was glad the pregnancy was over and wanted no more. Could Dr. Mercer help? He prescribed a device called a diaphragm that he said was "mostly effective." Well, I didn't care much for the "mostly" part, but it was better than sleeping with one's feet in a crock, as Ma had once advised.

Cole was called back to work on road construction, leaving me at home with three children. Sometimes Mother Morgan dropped by for a short visit, usually bringing fresh churned butter or a small pail of milk. Sometimes the neighbor with the telephone would drop over to gossip or borrow something. Otherwise, I was on my own.

Cole changed that summer. I had always thought that, even though he was hot-headed and self-centered, that he cared for us. I mean, cared for me and for the children. And maybe he did. But that summer there were weekends when he didn't come home, and some weeks when no part of his paycheck made it home either.

I knew better than to question Cole but, one evening, after supper, when the house was quiet and I was longing for a little closeness, I spoke. I told Cole that I missed him on the weekends and that the children needed their father's presence.

He told me he had found someone else.

"Her name is Lou and I met her up north. I'm telling you this because you asked, and I believe in honesty."

I was stunned. I hadn't asked any such question. I didn't want to know.

"No, don't tell me…"

His smile was the tight cruel smile of an executioner.

"Listen, Amy. I pride myself on being an honest man, and I'm going to tell you this. I won't sneak around to meet her or anyone. I'm telling you up front. She just hit me like a ton of bricks. I was with her those weekends I didn't come home."

"You found someone… important?" I was thinking of those one-night-stands neither of us talked about, the ones who left earrings in his car and makeup on his shirts. "Are you leaving me and the children, then?"

"I never said I was leaving. She has a husband and children of her own. He's dying of something and just can't keep her happy."

I wanted to know how he met her. This time, I did ask.

"I met her at a bar in Bad Axe. Me and the guys went to this place when we were working on the M-53 job. One night she just walked in, bought a beer at the bar and sat down at our table. She's just a medium looker, but full of smiles and jokes. She said right off that her husband was sick and that she had climbed out a window to get away. He watches the doors, she said." Cole laughed.

"So you're going to keep seeing this...Lou? What about us? Don't you owe us something?"

"Well, you got something. There's the house, I buy the groceries here. What more do you want?"

"Maybe I want a husband and a father for our children." I was pushing it, and I knew it, but how much was I supposed to take?

"You don't want a husband, you want a meal ticket. I can't remember when you tumbled with me the way Lou does. You're just, well, just a teacher. Lou's more of a..."

"More of a whore?" I dared him to react and he did, pitching the chair he had been sitting on into the wall and grabbing me by one arm. He turned my arm just so, just a little, until it was behind my back, held firm.

"Don't you ever call her that, Amy." The words hissed in my ears. "She's a good woman, a good mother. We hit it off. Don't make your own life worse by not understanding that. This is my life, and I will live it my way. She treats me good. She doesn't curse me, like someone I could name."

He slammed out of the house, and I heard gravel hit the side window as he wheeled out of the driveway. I rubbed my twisted arm in the silence until the baby began to cry. There were the children to think about. I would think about them and about the house, until there was no room left for thoughts for some tart named Lou.

Chapter Nine

Pa gave up the farm and moved in with Ivan. The farm wasn't much, anyway, a big step down from the productive lands he and Ma had rented after Crane. But with Ma gone, he said he didn't have the heart for it, and the work was just too much for a man his age. He invited Ivan, Connie, and me to take such of Ma's things that we could use. It was hard for me to speak up to Pa and tell him "I want" this or that, particularly now. So at first I kept quiet and Pa gave me the day bed, practically worn out, and a rocking chair with rockers broken off. They may not have been much but they matched what I had and we owned them and used them a long time. I had very little kitchen ware and did speak up about that. Among the things I chose was a blue granite baking pan that Ma had used for corn bread and cobblers. It so reminded me of Ma, and I valued it for that. In the end, most of Ma's kitchen items came my way. Connie had newer, matching pots and pans and Ivan's wife, Marjorie, didn't like used kitchen things.

Ivan and Marjorie farmed in Plainfield, not so far away, where Pa would have the spare room.

Hardly a month went by before Marjorie began finding fault with Pa. His work on the farm was less than expected, he was slow, he ate too much and snored loudly enough to shake the house. I had never liked Marjorie with her sharp tongue and off-putting ways and this latest just justified those feelings. I worried that Pa would end up without a place.

Pa came by one afternoon with totally unexpected news. He was getting married.

"Before you say a word, Amy, let me say my piece." He sat on one of the chairs in the dining room and I sat, too, holding the questions he knew I had.

"This isn't a dishonor to Ma," he said. "I know it's not been two years yet, but there are reasons." He looked at me, and I saw how tired he was, how suddenly old. I waited.

"The arrangement with Ivan isn't working. While I was thinking what to do next, I met this widow at Plainfield church. She was visiting there…her farm is in Dansville…and we exchanged words. I got to thinking about her, alone on that farm, and decided to pay a visit. Well, after awhile we came to an agreement. I would come and work the farm for her and tend the few animals she still has. In order for me to do this, she said, we had to get married. To her mind, no respectable widow shares her house with a man unless they are married. So I agreed. Her name's Lucinda Graymore. Most folks call her Lucy. She's pleasant to be around, has three married children and knows about mine. You'll like her."

This was a long speech for Pa and the first time he ever explained himself to me. My initial resistance faded into relief. He had found a new haven, and I didn't think Ma would begrudge him that. It didn't take long for me to welcome and appreciate this stepmother. She, in turn, welcomed all of us for afternoons and dinners on the farm. Pa had a new team of horses to care for, fields to till, and lambs in the spring. He was happy again, and years lifted from his face.

Catherine was doing well in school, her asthma attacks infrequent but fierce. Her worst attack came after Alice took her horseback riding on Star. We thought Catherine might be allergic to horses. Looking back and remembering Catherine's nervousness around large animals, I wonder if it could have been that fear, not Star that was the trigger. Either way, there was no more horseback riding for Catherine.

Alice got married and was now Mrs. Ted McDonald. She continued to teach school and Ted worked the family farm. I was pleased when they settled in a rented place nearby.

As for Cole, he was still seeing Lou. About every other weekend he drove to Harbor Beach, where she lived with her dying husband and three school-age children. These absences quickly became part of my own routine, and I filled the time with my own plans. There wasn't much I could do without a car, but we could visit Mother Morgan and walk downtown. Sometimes Alice would drop by and take us for drives. The worst part was the money. Lou was an expensive hobby from my view, as I saw the grocery budget shrink and house payments go past due. Cole was still selling Indian "relics" but the money he had said would come "our" way was rerouted to Harbor Beach. On my own I applied for welfare, got it and Cole's pride be hanged.

Lou's husband died. I took that as good news, thinking that some of the money Cole spent on tourist cabins every other week end might trickle back home. Cole had another idea. He would rent an apartment and move Lou and her children 150 miles south. Lou's new address would be in the next village east of Wolffton, a mere five miles from our home. Cole's purpose was to save his travel time and costs. I wondered about money to be gained from the sale of Lou's northern home and had a good suspicion whose pocket would be filled. At any rate, someone would have to pay rent and utilities and for the Brooks Brothers suit Cole bought to wear to Lou's husband's funeral.

Sometimes Cole and Lou would quarrel and he would come home at unexpected hours. He would just walk in, usually in a black mood, and ask about food. "What's for supper?" "Any pie left?" If I served him without comment, his mood would lift and the day could be saved. Sometimes he would take us for drives around the area, still looking for mounds or sandy hills where relics might be found.

The children liked these drives, although four-year-old Joseph would sometimes gaze uneasily through the windows from his vantage point between Cole and me, note the unfamiliar terrain and ask, in tremulous voice, "How are we going to get home?"

Once in awhile Cole would stop at the Vantown store or another country place and buy cheese, or pickled bologna. Cole would cut chunks with his pocket knife and everyone would eat as we traveled. Those excursions were often the highlight of the week and the family's main recreation. In the evenings following these good days, I prayed that Cole and Lou would quarrel more often.

Chapter Ten

"Dear Lord, please don't let me be pregnant again." It was the winter of 1941 and Cole and I had been married fourteen years. I prayed and hoped, but if I was looking for a sign, none was given, and the truth stirred in my belly.

It was another cash-poor winter. What money there was came from Cole's stones and fur trapping. Cole trapped for muskrat and mink in the Morgan swamp, this year extending the trap line to more than thirty traps. He checked them every day to reset sprung or frozen traps and to harvest any catch. Sometimes he checked twice a day, knowing that a muskrat, given time, would gnaw off its own caught leg and escape. It was miserable, cold work. This season, for reasons unknown, turned out to be unusually bountiful and Cole returned nearly every day with muskrats and, once in awhile, a mink.

I never understood why the Morgans so prized their swamp. It covered several acres behind and downhill from the farmstead. Its soggy edges were rimmed by pasture and railroad, and extended eastward to the first road beyond the village limits. Elderberry bushes, cattails, willows, and climbing vines grew there, along with who knew what else. Come spring, colorful buttercups and flags would bloom in the mucky shallows and frogs would sing their throaty songs. As pretty as it was then, it was treacherous all year long, its seemingly shallow water concealing murky black holes and pits large and deep enough to swallow a horse. I had walked the trap line one time with Cole…seeing him plunge hip deep through shattered ice was enough for me. I stayed away.

When the day's harvest was good, as it was this day, Cole's mood would be high, too. Spreading newspapers on the kitchen floor, he would skin each animal and stretch its hide over a wire and wood frame. This was something of a messy and smelly process and Catherine would invariably disappear upstairs. Joseph, not yet five, was curious about the furry animals and insisted on watching, as long as he was not too close. I held him safely on my lap so he could see.

Sarah wanted to watch, too, and watch she did, her little head sometimes getting in the way of Cole's work. Surprisingly, Cole was amused, rather than irritated, and said she could "help." Sarah wasn't quite seven and too young, I thought, to be handling knives, but she listened, and watched and Cole was pleased. She helped carry the stretched hides upstairs where they were hung to dry on a wire strung above the stairwell. The pelts, with their gamy, spoiled grease smell, would unavoidably hang in the children's upstairs bedroom space for days or weeks, until Cole took the dried pelts to the fur buyer.

Overall, this had been a successful day. It seemed a good time to tell Cole the news and after the children were in bed, I said the words.

"Cole, I have something to tell you." He looked at me from his chair, over the magazine he was reading.

"I'm pregnant."

"You're lying." He tossed the magazine aside and stood.

"I don't know what happened, Cole, I always used the…"

Now he kicked his discarded magazine and came toward me, his face angry.

"You did this on purpose, didn't you? You'd just do anything to break up me and Lou. You said it was safe. The doctor said it was safe."

"This was not deliberate, Cole. Do you think I want another child when it's a struggle to feed three? Do you think I enjoy cold rooms, no running water, and a husband who spends what little we have on someone else?"

Cole wasn't listening.

"Get rid of it. Just get rid of it. I told Lou I wasn't sleeping with you. I had to tell her that or she wouldn't... now here you are, making me out a liar. Get rid of it."

Cole stormed out of the house. His words stunned me, and I rubbed my forehead as if to erase their echoes from my mind. His reaction to earlier pregnancies had never been as explosive. Babies were a part of marriage and I thought he accepted that.

Sitting there, in my quiet house, the children asleep, I felt glad Cole was gone. As disloyal as such a thought was, I admitted to myself that I was relieved, thankful that Cole had taken his anger into the night instead of aiming it at me. There were worse things than being alone.

As I sat there, trying to forget Cole's words, my thoughts turned to that overheard conversation between Ma and Pa when she was pregnant with Davey. But then it was Ma that wanted out and Pa who said "no such thing."

Now I said it. I said it aloud. "No such thing." From this marriage to Cole, all I had, really, were the children. My whole marriage had been spent bending away from my own needs and wants toward his, giving in to whatever he demanded. Now all those years of bending and sacrifice had come to this. Cole was demanding that I give up our unborn child. The thought was a hellish burning in my heart.

What could Cole do when I refused? Leave us and move in with Lou? Turn our family into that "other" family he visited now and then? So be it. He was already a half-time husband and father. There was nothing he could do about my decision, and that thought, in itself, was pleasing.

I would keep my child.

Chapter Eleven

That would not be the last conversation Cole and I had about this pregnancy. He recognized, almost immediately, that I would do nothing to end it. Now he said we should give the baby away. He repeated this idea at least once a week, offering all kinds of reasons, most of which were veiled threats.

We couldn't afford another child. He wouldn't "be responsible" for what happened if I didn't agree with him. Lots of people wanted babies and would likely pay the doctor's bill. If he left all of us, how would we get by then?

As chance would have it, Alice was also pregnant and she could hardly wait to tell. I listened to her joyous news and then shared my own. I told her the things Cole had said, and the pressure I felt.

At first, Alice said nothing. She was thinking, mulling it over in the quiet way she had. After a few moments, she said only, "I'll talk to Mother." She squeezed my hand and departed. I could hear the eggbeater sound of her car as she made her way up the hill to Mother Morgan's.

I don't know what was said, but I do know that Mother Morgan talked to Cole and that he was somewhat subdued after that. Cole listened to no one, and he would tell you that he took no one's advice. Why he sometimes made exceptions for his mother was a mystery. I would have liked to own a little bit of her magic and wondered about it, but, as curious as I was, I asked no questions lest I break the spell. The change was a welcome relief.

Alice dropped by a week after we had talked. She told me she and her husband, Ted, had talked about our "situation." They were willing to take and raise the baby if we had to give it up.

"It would be kind of fun," she said, "Having two babies just months apart."

Dear Alice, ten years younger than me, once again extending herself to family. I felt tears running down my cheeks. I thanked her and said I appreciated the offer and would think about it. I also told her I wouldn't tell Cole just yet. Could this be just between us?

Her baby, a daughter, was born in early summer. I had three months to go.

When my time came, it was Catherine who walked across the road to telephone Dr. Mercer and Alice. Then she took Sarah and Joseph and walked them up the hill to Mother Morgan's. The two would stay there for the night.

When Cole arrived home from his day on road construction, he wanted supper. I could have prepared something, I suppose, in spite of strong contractions, but Catherine said she'd fix something for all of us.

While this was going on, Alice arrived. Cole set a basin of water on the cook stove to heat, and Alice filled the tea kettle. Cole's water was for his bath. Alice's was for the baby.

When Dr. Mercer arrived, Cole was taking his basin bath in the kitchen. He had brought fresh clothing, including his suit, from the bedroom where I now lay in labor. It was Friday and he was in a rush to begin his weekend with Lou. It seemed she had generously forgiven Cole for impregnating his wife.

I heard Dr. Mercer say to Cole that the delivery would be soon. I couldn't hear his response but heard Alice's voice, her tone unusually loud and firm, "You can wait."

The baby was a girl. Cole and Alice came in to see her, Cole to say that he was leaving. Even in these circumstances, I couldn't help but notice how handsome he looked, standing there in his suit and tie.

"Go ahead, give her a kiss," Alice urged, and Cole, looking a little uncomfortable, said, "We're past that sort of thing." I suppose his words were true, but they stung just the same.

After Cole left, I asked Catherine what we should name this baby, and we discussed our choices. Catherine liked Emily, and I liked Marie, and so she was named Emily Marie.

Alice spent the next several days running back and forth between her place and ours. She cooked and showed Catherine baby care basics. When she said to me, "So you've named her," and I nodded, we both knew a decision had been made. This beautiful Emily Marie would remain with me.

We didn't know it then, but Emily's birth was a mere two months before the bombing of Pearl Harbor. Manufacturing plants were already preparing for war and Cole got a job tooling airplane propellers at a Lansing factory. This was Cole's first non-seasonal regular employment since our marriage. He was soon reassigned to plant protection where he wore a uniform and badge, leather belt, and holstered gun. The uniform was a state police look-alike and Cole was impressed. Pa said that this had to be just the job for Cole—dressed up all day, himself on display and no dirty work.

Because of changing work schedules, Cole was required to have a telephone. That's how our first phone came to be fastened to the wall in the dining room, somewhat higher than I would have liked for easy reach to the mouthpiece. But the telephone wasn't for me, anyway, and Cole was taller. When I used the telephone, I just bent the mouthpiece's flexible neck downward as far as it would go. There was a long cord on the receiver…no trouble with that.

When the attack on Pearl Harbor came on December seventh, we heard the news by radio; newspapers followed. Great dread, uncertainty, and fear filled the air, raising a general mood of impending disaster, maybe the end of the world.

Even so, it was the Christmas season. Dire news reports were interspersed with Christmas music. Nativity scenes were placed and Christmas trees decorated.

Pa came with a carload of gifts that Christmas. He brought something for everyone and a shower of gifts for me. Never had I received so many wonderful gifts. There was a set of dinnerware, beautiful flowered plates and cups, the first complete set of dishes I had ever owned. There was silverware to go with it. In another box was a chenille robe, satin nightgown and slippers. The last package held a black winter coat trimmed with mouton lamb, a coat so splendid that I gasped when I saw it.. At the bottom of the box lay black velvet boots edged in fur. All this array of luxury was dizzying. What had gotten into Pa's head? He was a thrifty man with little means who gave small gifts, when he gave them at all. I didn't know what to make of it, what to say. . . I stole a glance at Cole, expecting a scowl or his usual comment about being-able-to-provide, etc., but he was smiling. I smiled back, overwhelmed. Then I saw Cole wink at Pa and knew that this generous gifting was no surprise to Cole. Pa, as usual, had gotten around Cole by including him in the planning.

On New Year's Eve, Cole was working second shift. The children and I were at supper when the telephone rang. I bent the mouthpiece downward and answered. It was one of my step-mother's daughters, Josie, calling to tell me Pa was dead. A stroke had taken him only hours earlier.

I asked her to repeat her words. Maybe I had misheard. After Josie told me again, I hung up the phone and tears flowed as I told the children what Josie had said. Now we all cried. Pa was loved by them, as well as by me.

There was nothing to do except call Cole and wait.

In those minutes and hours, I thought a lot about Pa and my years growing up. I thought about this most recent Christmas with its overabundance of gifts. I wondered if Pa had a premonition.

When we went to Pa's farm, or I should say, Lucy's farm, later, Josie said to me, about Pa, "He came here with nothing, and he left with nothing."

At the time, her words seemed cold, not at all comforting, until on second thought, I asked myself, *Isn't that what we all do?* and answered the question myself, *Pa doesn't need things, anymore.*

PART THREE

Finding My Own Way

As it turned out, it was not much more work having four children than three. Catherine was like a second mother to Emily
and when Catherine took a break, Sarah stepped in. Our Emily
had three mothers and a brother. Oh yes, a daddy too, part-
time, anyway.

Cole got a draft notice. Now that the country was at war, any
male between ages eighteen and forty could be drafted into mil-
itary service. I was worried that Cole would be taken, even at
age thirty-five with four children. How well I remember the day
of his army physical and his return that evening. He had been
rejected because of flat feet, was classified 4F, and was unlikely
to be called. We were all elated and relieved and a celebration
seemed in order. Cole sent Catherine and Sarah downtown to
buy ice cream. I hugged him and he smiled and hugged me back.
That was a great evening.

Before long, Catherine was in high school. She was a serious
student who rarely brought work home. "The work's so easy," she
said, "I just get it done in class or during study hall." Her grades
would easily get her into nursing school, a goal she had set for
herself. Nursing was a viable alternative, she said, after discover-

ing that she hated bookkeeping, shorthand and typing. I encouraged her while silently wondering how to pay the tuition. Time seemed to be rushing by.

I began to think about returning to work. But how could I? The task seemed beyond me while the thoughts stayed with me day and night. With no help in sight, I turned to prayer.

"God, help me. Please help me. Show me a way out of this poverty-ridden life." One night, as I lay alone in my bed, beseeching God one more time, an answer came. The words, spoken in the dark, spoken in my head, were, "Amy, help will come. Watch, pay attention, and act."

One day two people came to the door saying they were looking for a teacher for their rural school. I knew my certificate had expired and I told them I couldn't do it. I thought about that offer a long time after I closed the door.

So a week later it seemed strange, indeed, when two others came to the house with a similar offer. They represented a different rural school but their search was the same. When I said my certificate had expired, I was told it could be renewed with a few college credits. My heart leaped and I asked them to come back the next day.

Cole warmed to the idea, and we talked about what the extra money could buy. I wanted running water and inside plumbing. He said more money would help with utilities and home repairs. I said we needed better furniture and then, perhaps, Catherine's tuition.

I signed a contract to teach the following year at the Harker school a few miles south of town. It took all summer to get the "few college credits" I needed, but get them I did and was ready when September came.

On school days I drove the family car, Cole's car, and he drove a construction company pickup truck. It hadn't taken long for Cole to grow restless in the confining plant protection job. Seeing that the war effort was creating construction jobs everywhere, Cole went back to what he knew best and when his employer won bids for work at a bomber plant to be built at Ypsilanti, he was elated.

"Big job, Amy," he told me. "More money, too, that's the main thing. Them Japs are about to improve our life."

It wasn't the actual manufacturing plant that Cole and his crew were called to work on. The plant needed a massive network of roads, curbs, and sidewalks and huge drainage systems. Cole's crew was only one of hundreds, maybe thousands, who worked seven days a week to complete the entire installation in record time.

Sometimes Cole stayed in Ypsilanti all week, saving rationed gasoline and, he said, preserving his energy for the demanding work.

On weekends, Cole took the car and left the pickup with an admonition that I was to use it for emergency only. I was not to drive where the vehicle might be recognized, and I needed to replace what gasoline I used. Learning to drive that pickup truck was nerve-racking at first, but I was determined. Actually, the thing wasn't that much different from a car, it was just taller, wider, and longer, way too much of a monster to ever parallel park. But the vehicle gave us wheels and, over the summer, lots of little "emergencies" popped up on weekends. Some Saturday afternoons it seemed urgent that the children and I pile into the truck and go see a movie in one of the neighboring towns.

When school began that fall, Cole said I would have to pay him if I wanted to drive the family car to school. I shouldn't have been surprised, knowing Cole's propensity to turn a dollar wherever he could, but I was caught off guard. The little voice in my head said, "*So this is the way things are going to be,*" but all I said to Cole was that the amount seemed high. He said he wanted to be fair and lowered the fee a little.

This was a great time of change for all of us and it certainly took off in fits and starts. Catherine, Sarah and Joseph all took part in household chores and in caring for Emily. Minor chores like washing dishes and making beds were the least of it. There was wood and coal to bring in for the stoves, cooking and baking, water to pump for cooking, bathing and drinking; laundry to wash, ironing to do.

The way these children took on such an assortment of duties was a blessing to me. They went to school, I went to school. The rest of the time we worked at home. Oh, there were squabbles among the children as the household changed gears, but mostly not.

Supper was the heart of the evening. After our various labors and trials throughout the day, it was our time to be together. And, if the experience was not always enjoyable, it was, at least, obligatory. Our dining table was round, a big black thing that Cole had gotten in some trade or other. With its design of radiating lines from center, it reminded me of a clock, with Cole sitting at noon. Catherine sat at two o'clock, Emily at four, and I at six. Joseph's chair was at eight and Sarah's at ten.

Cherry pie was Cole's favorite and, when cherries were in season, the children would pick them from our trees and a pie would be baked. And so it was that a cherry pie was served one evening as a surprise for Cole. With a little show of fanfare, Cole took a bite and made exaggerated sounds of approval. His next mouthful included a cherry pit which he promptly plucked from his mouth and threw across the table at me. It hit my cheek and fell to the table where I let it lay. I didn't react—it was Cole's habit to target me with pits, bits of bone, stems, or anything in his food that he deemed inedible. I looked at my plate and said nothing.

"Hey, Amy," he said, and laughed.

"That's not funny, Daddy." Sarah, who had seen this act before, made the comment.

"Sure it's funny," Cole said, "I'm laughing."

I looked up, afraid that Cole would send Sarah from the table for her impertinence, yell at her, or worse. All of the children, except Emily, had felt the sting of his hand or belt. Sarah was looking at Cole, unsmiling, her chin up. Defiant, I thought.

"I don't think it's funny," she said.

"Is that so?" Cole asked. He raised himself a little, as if to stand up, apparently thought better of it and settled back down.

"Is that so?" he asked again. "Well, from now on I'll decide what's funny around here." He took another bite of pie, and we finished the meal in silence. I moved the errant pit to my saucer and thanked our lucky stars that Sarah had been spared this time.

On a Friday soon after, when Cole was preparing to go out, he examined his suit and found wrinkles. He took the trousers from their hanger and tossed them in my lap.

"Here, press these, will you? There's just a few wrinkles."

His tone was mild, off-hand. Not an unusual request, his tone said, "Just do your job."

"It's been a hard week, Cole," I said. "I'm just not up to it."

"What does that mean, 'not up to it'? You better get up here and do your job. Don't you always press my clothes?"

"I used to," I said, "Not any more. I'm done." I closed my eyes and leaned back in my chair.

I felt Cole whisk his trousers from my lap and heard him call Catherine. "Catherine, here's a job for you. I need it done now."

Cole showed her how trousers should be pressed and she did as he instructed. After that night, I never pressed his gadding-around clothes again.

Chapter Two

The money I paid Cole for using the family car made a big dent in my paycheck. Almost as much, I told myself, as a car payment. If I had to pay the money anyway, wouldn't it be smarter to have something to show for it?

At the local bank, I asked for Mr. Parks. He was no stranger to me or anyone in town. His smile was friendly and his manner pleasant when I saw him at church or the general store. Today I saw another side of Mr. Parks.

He looked at the paper I had filled out and shook his head.

"We're sorry, Mrs. Morgan," he said in a voice that sounded almost like sorry is supposed to sound. "You have no credit with us, no credit with anyone, and only very recent employment. Would your husband sign? It's our policy not to lend to married women without their husband's signature."

He looked at me with questioning eyebrows raised and I shook my head. "Thank you, Mr. Parks," I heard myself saying. "Thank you for the information."

This town was either the village of coincidences or grapevines, judging from what happened next. I visited the community library, as I did every week, and it seemed the librarian could hardly wait to tell me how a friend of hers had borrowed money from a local farm widow.

"Dorothy was so thrilled," the librarian said, "Of course her husband would have been glad to sign at the bank, but the bank wanted bigger payments."

I listened and, in time, the librarian mentioned the widow's name and told me she lived on the Wilson farm just west of town. I had seen this place many times, with its weathered barns and large house. Now, as I turned into the driveway, I looked at the house again. Big enough for a family of twelve, it now housed only one, the Widow Wilson, according to the librarian. Mrs. Wilson answered my knock promptly and invited me in without hesitation. She was very old and frail-looking but her eyes were quick and piercing as she gave me the once-over. I told her my name and why I was here and she nodded.

"Let's sit in the kitchen," she said, "I'll make some tea."

She wanted to know about my family, where I worked and what I wanted the money for. Her husband had known the Morgans, she said, or some of them. "Never were friends, though," she added, with a flash of the eyes that might have reflected a story or two. Then she went to another room and brought me the cash I asked for. She took a paper from a drawer, filled in some numbers and asked me to sign. I signed and thanked her.

"When you come to repay," she said, "We'll visit more. I don't get out much and like the company."

So I bought a used car on my own, without Cole even knowing. He asked where I got the money. "Borrowed it," I said, with no intention of telling him how or where.

"Just don't forget it's your debt," he said, "Your debt is not my debt."

Catherine was now a high school senior and had applied for admittance at Lansing's Edward W. Sparrow hospital nursing

school. She concentrated on her studies, striving to make valedictorian and ace the classes important to nursing. This was a
tense and busy year. Once in awhile she and her classmates would
overnight at each other's homes, sometimes to study, sometimes
not. Her friend, Bonnie, was there one evening when we gathered
for supper.

Catherine wanted to talk about school events and her plans.
Joseph, sitting across the table from her and bored, began making
faces. When a mouthful of mashed potatoes bloomed from his
lips like bubble gum, it was just too much for Catherine.

"Oh for heaven's sake, Joseph," she said, "Don't you have any
manners at all?"

Cole's head came up in animal-quick alert, his eyes flashing as
he looked at Catherine. Without a word, he raised his arm and
backhanded Catherine in the face.

"You're not in charge at this table," Cole said, "Now keep your
mouth shut."

Catherine stood up, in tears, blood showing on her mouth.

"Sit down," Cole said, "I'll tell you when you can leave."

Catherine stood there a moment, made a decision, and pushed
her way behind Bonnie, Emily, and me and raced upstairs. I was
on my feet, too, moving toward Cole before he could follow
Catherine. He was already standing when I took those few steps
around the table. His face was livid.

"Let her go, Cole," I said, putting one hand on his arm. "She
didn't mean anything. Just let her go this time."

He turned his face toward mine and I could see the rage still
there. Then, as quickly as it came it faded. The tightness in his
shoulders eased and he sat down. I sat, too, and we finished our
supper. Bonnie sat through it all, never saying a word.

After this, the relationship between Catherine and Cole
would never be mended. She would ever after call him "Cole,"
never Dad, or Father. She had shut him out.

Years later, when Catherine herself was past middle-age, she wrote about her father, "He believed, and taught us, that to be a Morgan was to be better, smarter than everybody else...this in spite of the semi-poverty in which we lived, and in spite of the fact that he, himself was a school dropout. And for some reason, we believed it, at least I did, and belief in one's self is not a bad thing to have. So he gave me that."

Chapter Three

Cole agreed to pay half of Catherine's first year tuition. Catherine planned to work summers and tuition after the first year was negligible, but the upfront payment was not. Looking back, it wasn't so much money at all, but it seemed like it then. I told Catherine that we would find the money.

I knocked on Mrs. Wilson's door again. This time she had cookies to go with her good tea and we talked a while before I brought up the reason for the visit, besides paying the first payment on my loan.

"I wanted to be a nurse, myself, when I was young," she said, "but things were different then. My father wouldn't hear of it, so horrified was he at the thought of me viewing or touching unclothed male bodies." She raised her hands in a dismissive gesture and added, "You know how men are. And my mother didn't back me, her idea was for me to get married and have babies.

"But today Catherine has both this opportunity and a mother who supports her. It would be a shame, wouldn't it, if all this was lost because of a few dollars? We'll just add this extra to your car loan and adjust the payment."

Once again, she went to another room, brought me cash, and I signed a new contract.

"This means a great deal, Mrs. Wilson." I hesitated, not knowing how to express my appreciation without being maudlin.

"I know," she said. "Do you have a picture of Catherine?"

I didn't and said so but promised to bring one of her graduation photos my next visit.

Catherine was subsequently enrolled at Edward W. Sparrow hospital's nursing school. She set to work acquiring items on a "must have" list provided by the school, including sew-in name tags. I drove her to school myself that first day and left her in the dormitory that adjoined the hospital.

A layer of sadness settled over me as I drove home. I would miss Catherine tremendously, not just her presence and company, but her help at home. And yet, alongside the sadness and vastly outweighing it was relief, even elation, in the knowledge that she was beginning a new life. Catherine, at least, was out of Cole's reach.

As I turned on Main street toward home, I noticed a large van parked at the library. "American Red Cross" was painted on one side. I recognized it as the mobile x-ray unit that visited two days each year to offer free chest x-rays to all comers. The next day, when I visited the library, I stood in line and received my free x-ray.

The next month, I got a postcard from the American Red Cross advising me to see the doctor I had named when registering. He told me that the x-ray had detected a growth, or mass, in one lung and sent me to the Chest Hospital where a Dr. Strong would decide what to do.

I didn't tell Cole or the children about this turn of events. I was frightened enough and saw no value in scaring the entire family when nothing definite was known. I would wait to see what Dr. Strong said. Meanwhile, I taught school every day and helped the children adjust to Catherine's absence.

Dr. Strong told me that the x-ray clearly showed a tumor about the size of my fist. Maybe it was benign, maybe malignant. There was no telling at this point. Surgery was the way to find out, the sooner the better. He said I should telephone his office to schedule the operation.

Cole said I didn't need surgery, that I seemed perfectly healthy, and that doctors just told people these things to fatten their wallets.

"But it was on the x-ray, Cole," I said, "the x-ray showed that something's wrong."

"Well, I don't know what those pictures show and neither do you. It's just somebody's word. I don't think it's necessary, and if you do it anyhow, then you can just pay for it."

Neither Cole nor I had insurance for doctors and hospitals. When I telephoned the hospital with this information, I was told that installment plans were available. I scheduled the surgery, signed the paperwork and prayed that I would recover quickly and not lose income.

Cole spent the weekend before surgery with Lou. He said he was going to work Monday morning directly from her place and wouldn't be available to take me to the hospital. I could take the bus if I didn't want to use the hospital parking lot for my own car.

I could have driven my own car but I was afraid that I wouldn't be well enough to drive home after the surgery. Dr. Strong said the incision would be a large C beginning in the middle of my back and curving under my right arm as far as my breast. One or two ribs would be removed for better access to my lung. The doctor said I would temporarily lose strength and healing time would be long.

Normally, I would have asked Alice to drive me, but she was busy enough already. Her mother-in-law was ill and the main responsibility of caring for her had fallen to Alice. There had to be another way.

Cole still had the company pickup and two or three local members of his work crew often rode with him. I knew them all, father and sons, and the rest of the family as well, so I called one of the sons and explained my problem. If I drove the company pickup to the hospital and left it in the parking lot, could he retrieve it and return it to our house that day?

"Don't even give it a thought, Mrs. Morgan. Consider it done. Just leave the keys under the driver's seat." The warmth in his voice was a welcome sound and I thanked him for his help.

"No trouble at all," is what he said before hanging up. The words echoed in my mind, a sharp contrast to the "too much trouble," I could expect from Cole.

I made arrangements with a friend to pick me up when I was discharged. Glenna and her husband would drive me home.

It was difficult to leave Sarah, Joseph, and Emily home like that, but Cole would be there, after all, and school would keep them busy during the day. I hugged them one by one and told Sarah I knew she would do her best. "And, Sarah, remember to hold Emily's hand when you go trick or treating. You know how enthusiastic she is." Halloween was coming up while I was gone.

Dr. Strong said the surgery went as expected, and the tumor appeared to be benign. Further tests would be done to make sure.

Catherine visited the hospital, riding the bus cross-town from Sparrow. The weather was cold for October and she looked thin and worried in the light coat she wore. I had been saving to buy her a warm winter coat and told Catherine she would find the little stash in the bedside stand. Her face brightened as she folded the bills and tucked them in her pocket. She told me she had talked to Dr. Strong and that everything looked good.

When Alice showed up with Sarah, Joseph, and Emily, I was nearly overwhelmed. In spite of everything, Alice had found time for me. Sarah was carrying a bouquet.

"It's from all of us," she said, as she arranged the blooms in their vase. "We want you to get better soon."

By "all of us," I knew Sarah well enough to know that she was implying that the flowers were from Cole, too. I knew better, but said I was pleased that everyone was thinking of me and that I would be home in a few days.

Cole never did stop by the hospital during my ten-day stay.

It took me three years to pay for that little outing.

Chapter Four

The kitchen was in disarray when I got home from the hospital. I could see that Sarah and Joseph had kept the dishes washed and put away; that wasn't the problem. Two grinders, a tumbler, and a couple of buckets full of stones filled half the room. The floor was layered with stone dust and crisscrossed with shoe tracks. A bucket of cloudy water stood on the floor near the sink, the center of a now dry splash pattern. Hand tools lay in the sink in a slushy grit. While I was gone, Cole had moved his stone work from the unheated shed to my kitchen.

"I tried to clean it up, Mama," Sarah said when she came home from school. "But Daddy said I was in the way, and he just made more dirt, anyway."

All three children looked a little neglected, their clothes wrinkled and necks unwashed. Clearly, Cole had taken no helping role with them. Sarah had done the cooking, although she said Cole cooked venison steak one night.

We began a sort of clean-up. Joseph pumped water for washing the sink and other kitchen surfaces. We left the floor for last. I realized quickly that just using a broom or mop was beyond me. Every thrust of the mop sent pain across my shoulder and back. The mop seemed to weigh forty pounds and I could feel sweat running down my face.

"I can't do this now," I told the children. "We'll just let it go. Let's use the water for baths. Sarah, can you get the water heating?" Sarah filled the dishpan and set it to heating…easier since I had bought a gas cooking range…and dragged in the wash tub. One by one, the children bathed. Emily first, little and not so dirty. Then Joseph and Sarah. Dried and in clean clothes, everyone looked less forlorn. While I rested, Sarah emptied the water, leaving new splash patterns on the kitchen floor. She told me she would cook some macaroni for supper.

I was lying on the sofa, mulling what to do next, when Cole came home. I heard him speak to the children as he passed through.

Then he stood by the sofa. "Been home long?"

"A while. Since before the children got home from school."

"How long before supper?"

"Ask Sarah. Cole, what are you doing in the kitchen?"

"Same thing I did in the shed, but I've figured out some new tricks, some new ways with the stones. I'll be making better pieces from now on, more expensive pieces like banners and birds. When the M-78 job is finished, the boss is shutting down for the season. That'll give me plenty of time to…Amy, what's the matter? You look sick."

"I am sick, Cole. I just have no strength left. I wore myself out helping the children with baths this afternoon."

"I told you not to have that operation. Now you're worse off than you were before." He turned back toward the kitchen.

"Sarah, get your mother a glass of water." Sarah hastened to comply while Joseph and Emily set the table.

"Get a can of fruit from the cellar," Cole told Sarah. "We can't eat just macaroni."

Supper that night included macaroni and tomatoes, canned peaches, bread and butter.

"Very good, Sarah," I said, savoring a mouthful. "You're getting to be quite the cook."

She smiled, pleased.

Sarah and Joseph cleared the table unasked and washed the dishes without quarreling. I think they were as glad to see me as I was to see them.

Cole showed me the stone he had been working on.

"Bet you wouldn't believe this was just a block of slate a few days ago," he said, turning the blue slate bird stone in his hand.

"See these holes?" he asked, pointing out the angled holes at each end of the stone. "This hole drilling is what I've been working on. Starting with the electric drill is okay, but if the holes aren't angled right, or if they're too round the whole thing looks fake. So I hand drill and sand inside the holes like the Indians did."

He showed me the little holes, not quite round, not quite the same diameter all the way through. Cole was obviously pleased with himself and, while I didn't quite appreciate the fine points of what he was saying, I granted that he knew what he was talking about.

"Very nice, Cole," I told him. I held the little stone in my hand. It was cool, smooth as silk.

"It's smooth, isn't it? That's from the tumbler. Slate is fairly soft for stone and the tumbler just takes all the grinding and sanding marks off in no time. I mixed up a fine grit mix and lined the tumbler with pieces of rubber tires. This bird is the best relic I've made so far. All it needs now is a little 'aging' and it'll be ready to peddle."

"Do you think you could clean up the floor a little? That dust just tracks all through the house."

"I'd think you'd be more interested in the bird," he said. "These are pricey items–aren't you interested in the money?"

"Of course, Cole." I didn't say what I was thinking, that any extra money would likely not improve our standard of living as much as it would his and Lou's. Cole had already bought a newer car and said he was thinking of buying a cabin cruiser for vacations. Not for me and the children, obviously.

"Sarah, get a bucket of water and mop up this floor." He added, in a comment tinged with sarcasm, "the dust bothers your mother."

I heard Sarah say, "Joseph is supposed to pump the water," and Cole's response, "Just get it done. Joseph, you can help."

That night, when Emily got ready for bed, she was wearing an outfit I'd never seen before, a loose pajama made from an old cotton blanket Cole had won at the fair.

"What's that you're wearing?" I asked.

"It's my Halloween costume. Sarah made it for me to go trick or treat while you were gone. I was a chinaman with black wig and pigtail she made from yarn. I kept warm, too."

"But it's not pajamas, right?"

"No, but Mama, it's so warm and Sarah sewed it just for me. I like it a lot."

Why argue over a thing like that? Emily liked the thing, it kept her warm and happy. What else could one want? I kissed her good night and, downstairs, thanked Sarah for her work.

"It was easy, Mama," she said, smiling, "And we had fun. Emily got a lot of compliments."

I went back to teaching the next week. The hardest part was the driving. Steering around curves and turning corners pulled painfully at my healing incision and the sore muscles of my shoulder and back. The best I could do was figure out the route with fewest turns and keep to that.

Other times, when the children were with me, they would help with the corners. Sarah or Joseph would sit beside me and add their strength to turning the steering wheel. They seemed to enjoy it and it certainly helped me out. This went on for months. Finally, when the school year was almost over, I could feel my body becoming stronger. When I lost the pain, I knew I was on the mend.

The best part was the letter from the hospital. It said the tumor had been analyzed and was not cancerous. My health was in no danger.

Chapter Five

The year Joseph was ten, Cole insisted that he go with him into the swamp to check the trap line.

"He's too young, Cole," I pleaded, thinking of those deep pits that never quite froze solid and the seemingly solid ground that was just tufts floating atop swampy muck. "Don't you think that's a dangerous place for a boy?"

"Hell, no. Not Joseph, anyway. You know he's in the swamp every chance he gets. There's a half-dozen 'hideouts' he's pieced together out there. Look at it this way. Joseph is ten years old. It's time to make a man of him."

It was true that Joseph liked to explore the swamp in summer. More than once I feared him lost, never to return, when he was late for supper. But in summer you could at least see where you were stepping. In winter, the swamp was little more than a mine-field thinly concealed under an opaque shell of ice. One false step and a boy could drown.

So much for my objections and fears. Cole taught Joseph where the traps were located, how to bag any caught animals and reset traps. After that first season, when Cole was "too busy," Joseph often checked the line alone, filling me with fear for his safety. More than once Joseph came home half-frozen after breaking through the ice, his boots, trousers, and gloves frozen stiff. I told myself that my fears were exaggerated and arose from my own overwhelming dread of the swamp. Even so, I considered going with Joseph and would have except for the certainty that Cole would ridicule Joseph as a "mama's boy, wah-wah-wah".

Before his thirteenth birthday, Cole gave Joseph a .22 rifle and shooting lessons provided a new reason for swamp visits. Joseph was eager to learn new skills and proved a good student. Cole wanted to take him deer hunting.

When deer season rolled around, Cole told me he was taking Joseph on his annual deer hunting trip north. Some months earlier, Cole had salvaged a small house trailer from somewhere and parked it in the back yard. It was a wreck of a thing, off-kilter on its wheels, a door that wouldn't close. Cole said it was time Joseph learned something of carpentry and mechanics, and the two of them worked hours and evenings putting the little trailer in shape. It was entirely road-worthy when deer season arrived and I felt comfortable that Joseph would be safe on this new venture with his father. Cole picked a high powered rifle from his own collection for Joseph to use.

Cole said the rifles needed to be "sighted in," a process completed by the time I heard of it. Cole had taken Joseph, the rifles and ammunition into the Michigan cellar under the house and had fired at targets against one cellar wall. Was the man mad?

"Weren't you worried about ricocheting bullets?" I asked Cole.

He looked at me with a mixture of amusement and contempt.

"No, Amy, we shot with hollow points. There is no ricochet."

I wasn't convinced, but neither Cole nor Joseph bore shrapnel wounds, so probably he was right.

When Cole and Joseph rolled out of the driveway with the trailer in tow, I sent a prayer behind them for Joseph's safety.

A deer was lashed to the fender of Cole's car when they returned. Joseph seemed fine, although quieter than usual, as he hauled his duffel into the house and upstairs.

"How was your trip?" I asked Cole after the trailer was unhitched and the deer hung in the cold shed.

"Great, the trip was great. Joseph took to tracking and hunting right away, better than Albert. That kid's a klutz if ever there was one."

"Albert? You took Albert?" I knew from earlier conversations that Albert was Lou's son, about Joseph's age. Alarm was rising in my throat like sour milk boiling. "So you had two boys to look after?"

"You might say that. Lou was real good with both boys, real patient with Joseph's silence. I told her that was just his mother's influence."

"You took my son on a trip with that woman, slept together in a one-room trailer, and you didn't tell me?"

"Why should I tell you? You'd just get all flustered, like now, and stir up trouble. By the way, that's 'our' son. I am his father and I will do as I please where he is concerned. 'That woman', as you say, is a part of my life, and he needed to meet her. I want him and Albert to be friends."

"Friends? Now you're going to pick Joseph's friends? You're out of your mind." I was furious, so angry that I might have said more and caused calamity had I not walked away, outside the house, down the path to the privy. Without a coat, I didn't stay long, just long enough to level out my feelings. When I went back into the house, Cole was reading the newspaper.

This turn of events was a knife in my side. It stuck with me from that day forward, twisting whenever Joseph went anywhere with Cole.

Chapter Six

There was going to be trouble between Cole and Sarah. When Sarah was a little girl she had worshiped Cole, following him around, watching what he did and wanting to learn for herself. She had an independent streak that Cole didn't like and he had done his best to squash it or beat it out of her. Like the other children, Sarah was punished often, whipped with switches and Cole's belt, his razor strop and his construction worker's hand. The desired result, obedience, was achieved, for awhile. But by the time Sarah was a teenager, it was clear to me that physical punishments were like first skirmishes in a terrible war.

Sara's adoration had turned to fear, contempt, and a strategy of avoidance that we had all learned. She kept an arm length's distance when Cole's mood was dark and she complied with his requests and orders when they came. Even this compliance irritated Cole; he objected to her posture, the way she moved and, sometimes, the way she looked at him.

"What did she do? What did she say?" I asked Cole after he had slapped her hard. "She was just setting up the ironing board to press your pants like you asked." Sarah had inherited this task since Catherine left for school.

"Her insolence," he said. "She doesn't have to say anything. She has a way of being...I would say, silently sassy."

Sarah's defiance was generally low-key where Cole was concerned but it was always there. At school she resisted what she saw as unjust authority and warred against it. Like Catherine, she earned high grades, a ticket perhaps, to more leniency from teachers faced with her head-strong and determined ways. Sarah worked after school and some nights as switchboard operator at the local telephone company. There, as at school, she objected to overreaching rules and, surprisingly to me, got some changed. Her unwavering and piercing gaze was unsettling to many, including Cole.

Sarah only half-believed stories her school friends told about Cole and another woman until chance confirmed them. While at work, Sarah saw Cole and Lou in Cole's car, driving by the telephone office. She asked me if the woman was Daddy's girlfriend and I nodded. There was nothing I could do or say. The truth would have to suffice.

Sarah wanted to be in charge, and she was while I was teaching and she the oldest at home. When I arranged a credit account for her at the corner grocery, I knew I could rely on her to buy only good and necessary family food items. During the school year, I could count on Sarah having dinner in process when I came home. Joseph and Emily had their tasks too and did them. They said Sarah was bossy.

It was Cole's habit when coming home off the job to remove his sweat-stained and cement caked shoes, socks, shirt, and pants in the back room. He would leave them on the floor or on hooks, come into the kitchen in shorts and undershirt, splash his face and hands with water, proceed to his living room easy chair, and read the newspaper. Many times he would fall asleep before supper was ready. I would call him once, "Cole, supper's ready," and if he didn't respond, the rest of us ate without him.

That's what happened one night, when Sarah was about sixteen. After supper, I moved into the living room to correct class papers and the children cleared the table, leaving Cole's plate as was our practice. Cole's food would be reheated and served when he woke up.

The kitchen was cold, Cole said, when he awoke an hour later. He wanted warmth while he shaved and washed up at the sink before going out. I could hear him opening and shutting the oven and broiler on the stove, followed by clangs and curses. I lay my papers aside and started to get up.

"Never mind, Mama," Sarah said, "I'll go. He'll want supper, too. I can fix it."

Sarah walked into the kitchen to see the broiler pan, oven racks, and even the bottom oven tray scattered in front of the stove. I heard her laugh, and then Cole's roar.

When I got to the kitchen with Emily close behind, Sarah was standing with her back against the cupboard. She was silent, tears welling in her eyes as she removed her glasses and slipped them behind her on the counter.

I could see that Cole had hit her in the face. He raised his arm again.

"Please, Cole, don't," I said, putting my hand on his arm. Emily, half behind me, was crying noisily. Cole ordered her into the living room.

"You get in there too, Amy, unless you want some of the same."

Sarah raised both her arms, put her hands on Cole's raised arm and pressed down. I gasped, seeing disaster coming next.

"Not Mama," she said.

Cole's attention was immediately back on Sarah. She didn't let go, didn't look away. After a few excruciating moments, Cole dropped his arm and turned away. Sarah picked up her glasses and I could see a large red mark on her cheek and blood on her lip.

She didn't cry. Instead, she offered to light the oven so Cole could heat the kitchen as he was trying to do. She put the stove back together, reheated his supper, and I corrected my papers. When Cole was clean and shaved, fed, dressed in fresh clothes and backing his car out of the drive, we all breathed a sigh of relief.

Later, Cole would say that Sarah had swore at him and, perhaps, her laughter was the equivalent of cursing to his ears. Sarah went to school that week with a large, ugly bruise across one side of her face. Two of her teeth were loose. She wore her wounds like a warrior and told me that when asked about her injury, she said the truth flat out. No more half-truths or excuses for Daddy.

Her bruises healed and teeth tightened, but the memories of that attack remained raw for years, perhaps forever. Many years later she would tell me that she had learned two important things from her father that night. Stand your ground. Don't cry.

Chapter Seven

"Are you happy with the way your days are going?" Mrs. Wilson and I were sitting at her kitchen table, once more sharing tea and cookies. She had tucked away the loan payment I had brought and listened to my newest request. I wanted to add a bathroom and running water to the house.

I looked beyond her to Catherine's graduation photo, brought on the prior month's visit and now framed and displayed on the wall. In a way, it was like looking at my own younger face, unsmiling, observant. "There are times," I told her, "Times of happiness when I know why I stay. There are the children, after all, my greatest blessing. I would say that life is improving, becoming a little easier."

Mrs. Wilson had become more than a money lender, she was a trusted friend. Our monthly visits were refreshing exchanges that buoyed my spirits and confidence for days.

"Cole said he would do most of the work," I told her, referring to the bathroom project. "He agreed to pay half the materials if I paid for his labor. He pointed out it would cost me if I had to hire someone else."

Mrs. Wilson raised her eyebrows and gave a disdainful sniff.

"Does he pay you for cooking and housework? Were me, I'd just hire a local builder."

"I thought about it. It's not worth the aggravation of going against Cole. If I can get the work done, that's what matters. I am just so tired of walking to that privy. If we didn't have to pump all our water by hand and heat it…what a relief." I worried about Mrs. Wilson's reaction, fearing that she would turn down my request. I needn't have worried.

"Very well, Amelia," she said. "I can see you are determined to stay on this path. When you're ready to start the work, come back. Meanwhile, I'll be sure to have enough cash in the house. I am spending a lot these days," she added, with a smile. "And it's great fun, too, although I'm sure Mr. Wilson, may he rest in peace, would not approve."

On the drive home from Mrs. Wilson's, I thought about her question. Was I happy with the way my days were going?

A few things were clear to me: Cole would not change his ways. While I was not exactly used to Lou and the others, I had found ways to forget they were real. When Cole was home there was no need to think of them and, when he was gone, I did my best to squelch whatever mental images might come of him and someone else. There was a positive side too. The children and I had not just grown accustomed to his absences, we looked forward to them. To tell the guilty truth, those hours and days gave us the space and time to do whatever we wanted.

Cole's hard discipline of the children was a worrisome thing, and I prayed and trusted that they would grow up safely. When I had railed against his punishments, and threatened to end our marriage, Cole had said, "Just try it. I'll take Joseph and be out of here so fast your head will spin. Don't think you'll ever find me or Joseph. You won't." Those terrorizing words burned indelibly in my memory. I knew they were true.

There was the money too, sporadic as it was. The idea of supporting the family on just my salary was daunting. I could do more by using his money whenever it came my way. Better some-thing than nothing. I was biding my time.

The stigma against divorced teachers had faded and become less of an issue, but maybe a family headed by a strong, part-time father had its pluses. Would a broken family led by a woman who could never spank her children be an improvement?

Mrs. Wilson would say these thoughts were all rationaliza-tions to avoid change. She would say I was not "biding my time," I was dragging my feet and she would urge me to toss away my chains and put my fears aside. I thought about her comment on spending money, how it was fun and Mr. Wilson, may he rest in peace, might see it differently. A single life might be gratifying for her but, well, she had money.

I told myself that, mostly, I did not want to bring new calami-ties on myself and my children. Things could be worse. And yet, underneath it all, I think the chain that shackled me closest was the uncomfortable knowledge that I still loved Cole. He had been my first love, the flame—or so it seemed—that permanently fused my heart to his.

The new bathroom was added at the far end of the dining room. Cole tore down the wall between the kitchen and din-ing rooms, creating a more open area. He was not a professional builder or plumber but the result was good. I liked the way it looked. A happy bonus was that the last of Cole's stone grinding equipment was moved out of the kitchen and into the shed.

Cole also removed the hand pump from the outside well and pulled the pipe. The privy became a fusty storage shed.

There was money enough to have a gas furnace installed in the cellar. Now we got rid of the living room wood burner with its continual dirt and ashes. Not to mention the need to use my cooking range to heat the kitchen.

Cole's boss owned a lakeside cottage in western Michigan. He wanted Cole to build a boathouse there and said he also wanted the rooms at the cottage repainted. Cole said he and his family would do it and so it was that I became an unofficial employee of his construction boss. The children enjoyed the lake, I painted walls and ceilings, and Cole worked on the boathouse evenings and most weekends. For me, this was the closest thing to a vacation since I was a girl, and I savored each day. For Sarah, Joseph, and Emily, it was their first lake vacation. They splashed in the water, collected turtles and made near-shore excursions in an old rowboat, finding new adventures every day. Catherine intended to help with the painting, earn a little money for herself. Instead, she developed horrendous allergies to the oil-based paints we used and had to return home. Once the allergy subsided, she found summer work near school and didn't return to the lake.

Cole took us hiking along the banks of the Thornapple river, "exploring," he said. Cole was at his best, showing the children how to "Indian walk" and pointing out giant turtles in the river. He identified unfamiliar trees and plants, including those to avoid.

"See that hill?" Cole asked, as we rounded a curve in the river. It was a high sandy slope rising beyond the water's edge, nearly bare of vegetation. "That's the kind of place to look for Indian relics. Let's go."

We climbed and searched, sifting handfuls of sand through our fingers. Years later, I still cherished the arrowhead I found that day.

Joseph found an arrowhead, too, and slipped it quietly into his pocket after showing it to Cole.

This was a summer when we were a family again and I hated to see it end. In August, with the painting done and the boathouse built, it was over. We packed our things into Cole's car, locked the cottage and drove away. Emily watched through the back window until the cottage was lost to view.

After we got home, Cole took a small vase from his pocket. It was about five inches tall, with delicate handles. The pink iris and brown glaze I recognized as majolica ware. It was a nice piece and looked familiar. He handed it to me.

"Put it on the shelf," he said, "A reminder of our summer. The boss'll never miss it." He laughed.

I remembered then where I had seen it, on a corner what-not shelf at the lake cottage, left there by an employer who trusted us. Cole had said one time that this boss was like a father to him, more than his own father had ever been. I didn't mention the contradiction. Why spoil the moment or Cole's mood?

"Thank you, Cole, it's beautiful," is what I said. Now the vase stands on my shelf, an unscrupulous but pretty reminder of that rare and happy summer.

***

Come fall, with construction work winding down, Cole devoted more and more time to his stone making. His network of buyers, sellers, collectors, and, yes, other fakers, had expanded to three states. One collector he met was Ellen Salisbury. The recent widow of a wealthy businessman/collector, Mrs. Salisbury had inherited an extensive collection of Indian artifacts. Cole buttered her up as only Cole could do, bought a few of her less-expensive pieces, and became a trusted confidant.

Cole said, in a slightly derisive tone, that Ellen liked to think she knew about Indian relics and had decided she was qualified to eliminate the more common pieces from her husband's collection. She planned to replace them with rarer, more beautiful pieces. Well, you know where this is leading.

Several half-filled bushel baskets of stones sat in the kitchen, transferred from Cole's car by Cole, Joseph, Sarah, and Emily. There were axes and celts, mortars and pestles, spears, arrowheads, and who knew what else? Cole could hardly contain himself.

"All of this," he said, swinging his arm in an all-encompassing arc. "All of this for just that quartz banner I carved out. She liked it, said it was beautiful." He laughed. "Then she said, 'how can I be sure it's not a fake?' and I told her I'd prove it. I scrubbed it in the sink, ran hot water on it, and even used Old Dutch cleanser and steel wool. That baked varnish patina held, sure enough, proving it was genuine." Cole stopped to catch his breath. He picked up a stone from one basket.

"I can fix a lot of these so they'll bring more money. Even as is they're worth more than that piece of quartz I started with. Think about it, Amy, just think about it. Did you ever imagine you'd see the day when one of my pieces would be part of a collection as important as Salisbury's?"

The children were examining the stones, picking them up, putting them back. No one answered Cole's question, least of all, me. What I felt was fear that someday, someone would come knocking on the door asking if the relic maker lived here.

Maybe it was just as well that these ill-gotten gains would be siphoned off for Lou.

Chapter Eight

"Everyone else's parents are going to be there. Daddy's just being selfish and mean. I asked him straight out to come to my graduation. You heard me. And he just walked out the door." It was Sarah's graduation night and Cole had just left for another weekend with Lou.

"I'll be there, Sarah. Aunt Alice will be there." It was all I could think to say. I was tired of making excuses for Cole, and it was useless anyway. Sarah knew full well where her father was going. "Joseph and Emily will be there too."

"But I wanted Daddy to hear my speech." Sarah was giving the valedictory, as Catherine had done before her.

"Wipe your eyes, Sarah. This is your big night. Let's just forget about Daddy and enjoy it."

"All my friends will notice. I have a notion to just rewrite my speech and tell the whole town that my father isn't there because he's visiting his whore again. Not that most of them don't know about her anyway. I just hate him. He is so horrid to us."

"Well, Sarah, we need to do the best we can. Your cap and gown are hanging on the door. Just put them on and let's go."

The school gymnasium was brimming with students, their families, and most everyone else in town. We left Sarah at the staging area and found seats among the filling rows of folding chairs.

"Are these seats taken?" Harry Winter, manager of the telephone company where Sarah worked, and his wife, Jean, were looking for seats.

"No, no, please sit," I said, "There's just Joseph, Emily, and me."

Harry and Jean would be leaving town the following week. He had found a better position with a private telephone company up north and had offered Sarah full-time work as telephone operator. She would live with the Winters, rent free. Sarah, eager to explore life away from home, had accepted.

We exchanged pleasantries and waited. If the Winters wondered about Cole's absence, they kept their curiosity to themselves.

Emily was getting restless by the time Sarah was introduced as valedictorian. I held my breath, but only for a moment as she began to speak. There was no heated tirade against her father, only the rehearsed paragraphs she had written weeks before.

After the ceremonies, she joined us in the hall where she was warmly hugged by friends and teachers alike. The Winters hugged her too and said good night.

In a week, Sarah would be gone. Just as well, I told myself. The tensions between her and Cole were intense, a volcano building toward explosion. Did I worry about my seventeen-year-old daughter moving so far away with an employer we didn't know that much about? No, if anything, I thought she was safer there than at home. She may have been an unsophisticated small town girl, but she was neither starry-eyed nor helpless. I had seen Sarah turn people away under her green-eyed stare. With her sturdy country look, homemade dresses, and fierce defenses, I was confident she could take care of herself.

When the Winters stopped by with their car and trailer, Sarah was ready. Mr. Winter tucked her suitcase and sewing machine into the trailer and Sarah waved good-bye, leaving Joseph, Emily, and me on the porch waving back.

In a month, Catherine would graduate from nursing school and begin employment at a hospital in Detroit. That was a long distance away, and I reminded her that a job in Lansing would be closer to home.

"That's just it, Mother," Catherine had replied. "I don't want to be closer to home. It isn't you, you know that, but I just have to get away from his bullying." "His" of course, meaning "Cole's."

She was home for the weekend, and we talked while I took clean laundry from the clothesline in the back yard.

"Besides," she told me, "Tom and I are getting married. He's got a job near mine and both are near his folks."

Tom was an engineering student at Michigan State College, near the hospital where Catherine studied. We had met and he made a pleasant impression with his ready smile and soft way of speaking. Otherwise, I knew little about him except that his parents had emigrated from England, his father was an Episcopal cleric turned church executive, and Tom had been brought up in the city.

There was no need to ask, "Are you sure about this?" but I asked anyway.

"Of course, Mother, you know me. I wouldn't be doing this if I wasn't sure. I do love him, and I know he'll be good to me. He's smart, and there's not a mean bone in his body."

"But what about your career, your education? Is it all to be wasted, just tossed away?" In that moment, asking that question, an image of Ma flashed in my mind. She had chided me with a similar question twenty-some years earlier.

"It's not like that," Catherine said. "We'll both work. It takes two incomes to get ahead these days. My training hasn't been wasted. Actually, Mother, education is never wasted. You told me that."

Cole had some excuse ready for Catherine's graduation night, and she said she hoped he wouldn't have the same excuse to avoid walking her down the aisle. Catherine and Tom planned a small wedding in his father's church. Only family, a few friends, and church dignitaries were invited. Tom's parents were hosting the reception in their back yard, which meant a drive for us to the city. The idea of driving into Detroit filled me with dread and I hoped, hoped in my heart that Cole would drive us.

Cole said he saw no reason to walk Catherine down the aisle. Catherine, prepared for this response, was more persuasive than I had ever seen her.

"It's just that, if a bride's father is living, he walks her down the aisle. It's a traditional thing, and, of course, it's Tom's dad's church."

"Churchy people, not for me. Haven't been to church in thirty years, no need to go now."

"Tom's parents aren't 'churchy'," she insisted. "You'll like them. And the bishop will be there too. Wouldn't you like to meet a bishop?"

"Hell, no. Just plain people are good enough for me."

The discussion seemed stalemated.

"But you'll be the handsomest man there. The aisle isn't long, but it's long enough for everyone to see. I really want you to do this, just for me."

Well, that was her ace. And it worked. He agreed, "against his better judgment" to do this one thing.

So that summer ended with Catherine married, Sarah more than a hundred miles away, and a near empty house. Or it seemed that way. For the first time, each of the two upstairs bedrooms held one person. At least half the time the downstairs bedroom held only one, too, and sometimes, lying there alone, I let pictures from my imagination frighten me. I saw that our house was a pitcher and Catherine's and Sarah's lives were pouring out. Soon Joseph, then Emily, would follow, leaving the pitcher empty and hollow. What would I do then?

Chapter Nine

Now it was Joseph's turn to keep an eye on Emily while I was at school. Before I left in the morning for the five-mile drive to work, I would call, "Time to get up," from the foot of the stairs. I left it to Joseph to awaken Emily, get breakfast around, and get the two of them off to classes.

Joseph, almost sixteen, took supervision of his sister seriously. When Emily complained that he was too rough combing her hair in the morning, I suggested she comb it herself and let Joseph just do the finishing touches. He was not about to let her go to school looking like Little Orphan Annie. Joseph insisted Emily eat breakfast, a rule he did not always follow himself.

An old Ford sat in the yard, waiting for the driving permit Joseph's sixteenth birthday would bring. When Cole and Joseph had brought the car home it needed a little work, but it was complete now, down to the waxed exterior and scrubbed white-wall tires. Joseph had done most of the work himself with Uncle Ted's help. Alice's husband was well known for his farm mechanic's garage; he fixed tractors and motors as a sideline. Ted knew of Joseph's interest in all things mechanical and now took him in as a sometime apprentice. It was here that Joseph learned the ins and outs of "Ford-fixin'." If the few miles of country road between home and Uncle Ted's sometimes carried an unlicensed Joseph and his Ford-in-progress to Ted's garage, those in the community who kept an eye on such things, mostly neighbors and relatives, pretended not to notice.

Since that first foray into deer country, Joseph had spent more and more time with Cole. "How wonderful," some would say, "That the boy can spend so much time with his father." I chose to think of these comments as well-meaning and let them stand unchallenged. There was nothing to be gained through discussion.

Cole, now supervisor of his employer's main construction crew, hired Joseph when he was fourteen.

"It's time to make a man of him," Cole said, words I had heard before. "He needs to learn about real work, learn a skill."

Joseph saw the chance to earn money to buy a car. In fact, the money to purchase his little Ford-in-waiting, had come from two summers' work.

Cole began demanding more and more from Joseph. He was given harder tasks, heavier work and longer hours with no lee-way for error.

"No one's going to be able to say Joseph gets special treatment just because he's the boss's son," Cole said one evening after a run-in with his boss's new partner.

"Joseph does what I say, not what that s.o.b. Frank says. Frank doesn't know diddley about paving and he comes around telling me how to do my job. I just told him, 'Look, this is my goddamn crew and I run it my way. Just stay the hell out of my way, and I'll stay out of yours. And don't come around saying I'm too hard on my own son.'

"None of his damn business, anyway." Cole was furious, just remembering. "I don't know why the old man ever hooked up with this Frank. We were doing just fine without him, getting good jobs, keeping an eye on costs. Any more crap from him and I'll take it to the old man himself. Telling me how to treat my kid…"

I knew the work was tiring for Joseph. He was tall like Cole, but slender and still growing, probably sixty pounds lighter than his father.

"I don't expect anything more from Joseph than I expect of myself," he added, maybe thinking a little more about Frank's words.

"Maybe you do expect too much from a boy not quite sixteen," I offered, "He hasn't had your years on the road."

"Now don't you get into it, Amy. What do you know about building roads?"

There was no answer for that, and I let the question die of neglect.

Joseph, however, did not complain, saving his money and working on his car. His school grades were average, but at least he attended faithfully, and it was understood that Joseph would work with Cole after graduation.

That 1936 Ford was Joseph's pride and joy. He drove Emily to school, drove the village streets after school, and ventured into neighboring towns alone or with friends. His car and driver's license boosted his status among other hometown teens. This new attention brought out a more smiling, social Joseph. Sometimes he came home late. He had a girlfriend named Barbara in the next town.

When Joseph came home after ten o'clock, if Cole was home and awake, there was always a scene: Cole berating Joseph while Joseph listened. So Joseph figured out a strategy. When Cole waited up, he was always in his favorite chair, reading or watching the new television, the same chair where he often fell asleep, both before and after supper. Joseph figured that the noise and lights of his Ford might be waking an otherwise sleeping sentry. His strategy included turning off his headlights a half-block away, cutting the engine and coasting into the drive and his spot under the apple tree. He would tiptoe through the kitchen and upstairs while Cole snored in his chair. His tiptoeing didn't get by me; it simply said he was home, and I could now sleep more easily myself.

Ultimately the system failed. It was eleven o'clock on a Wednesday night when Joseph glided into the driveway, his timing coincident with Cole's bathroom visit. I heard the sounds and, sensing trouble, slipped into my housecoat. I was behind Cole when Joseph came through the kitchen door.

"Sneaking in, are you?" Cole sounded mild enough.

"Just being quiet, don't want to wake the neighbors."

"Or the old man, huh? There's work tomorrow, Joseph, in case you forgot. Morning comes early when we're pouring concrete and the day is long. How do you expect to give your best at work when you're staying out half the night?"

"It's still early, Dad. I'll be rested by morning." Joseph turned to go upstairs.

"Don't walk away from me when I'm talking to you."

Joseph stopped and waited, before speaking.

"You don't tell the other guys what time to go to bed. Some of them stay out lots later than this when we're on the road."

Cole took a step toward Joseph.

"You live in my house, you eat my food, you do as I say. Anytime you don't like that, just get out."

For a moment, Joseph was silent. Then he said, "Okay, I'll get some of my things from upstairs."

Cole was dumbfounded. He couldn't believe his ears.

As Joseph moved to collect his things, Cole recovered.

"Wait," he said, "Go if you want, get the hell out, but there's just one thing. You just leave that car here."

"It's my car," Joseph said, "I paid for it."

"You're not twenty-one. You're not even eighteen. You can't own anything. It's mine if I want it, and I'm taking it in payment for room and board around here."

Joseph's resolve collapsed in defeat. How could he go any-where without his car? How could he leave his most precious possession? He looked only moments away from tears.

"Cole, let's talk about this in the morning." It was the first thing I had said during the dreadful exchange. My words were more to divert Cole's focus than anything. Just delay further action, I thought. Give Cole time to forget, as he often did.

"Get the hell to bed." Cole's words were for me, but I didn't budge. "You too, Joseph," he added, and when Joseph was ascend-ing the stairs to his room, I went to bed myself. Cole turned on the television, and I listened to that background noise until I fell asleep. I heard Cole when he came to bed later, but neither of us said anything, not even, goodnight.

Chapter Ten

Another graduation picture hung on Mrs. Wilson's wall now, beside Catherine's and Sarah's. Joseph was graduating next month.

"Good looking young man," Mrs. Wilson said, admiring her gallery. "Your nest is emptying, Amelia."

I was making my final loan payment today, finally out of debt after a half-dozen or so borrowings. It felt good, but sad, too. I would miss these monthly conversations.

"Yes, and it won't be long before Emily flies. She's a teenager and, I must say, quite different from the others."

"She's the baby. Babies are always different." Mrs. Wilson smiled. "Tell me how."

"Well, to begin with, she has more friends than her sisters. Where Catherine and Sarah had three or four, Emily has ten or twelve. She's not as serious, either, wants to have fun and be with her friends instead of studying, reading, or working for money. Her grades at school leave something to be desired." I paused, thinking of the contrast. "I must admit, Mrs. Wilson, that her light ways are great fun for me. When she trundles all those friends home and fills the house with their laughter, I just laugh, too. She's the sunshine in my days."

"So you're spoiling her, then. Or is she spoiling you?"

"I never thought of it that way, but you could be right. And you know what? I don't care. If life doesn't have to always be serious and practical, why continue in it? This is the best time of my life."

"Well, good times sometimes need financing. Do let me know if I can help you there. Keep in touch, Amelia. I will keep you and your family in my prayers."

I drove away, thinking of Emily and Joseph and the days that lay ahead. These were mood-lifting thoughts.

———

Work wise, there were more troubling concerns. For months there had been talk about school consolidation. Thinkers of the day were pressing for larger, centralized schools rather than keeping students in their rural environments. My school, like most other country schools around the state, was eight grades. High school was offered at town schools, with "country kids" bussed in to join the "townies."

More and more country schools were closing, and I worried that mine would be next. Word was that only degreed teachers would be accepted in town, leaving certificate teachers, like me, unemployed. I still attended Michigan State every summer and seminars and night classes throughout the year, but it would be another year or so before I would earn my degree.

The idea of teaching in a larger school wasn't all that thrilling. As it was, I was in charge of my school, I dealt with parents and school board, disciplined students, kept the classroom clean and warm, even shoveled the snow if no student came forth.

With consolidation, I would teach one grade and, considering the influx of students, probably only a portion of that grade. There would surely be professional and social issues between teachers, and I had never been a particularly social person. I was there to teach students, not visit over lunch or commiserate about real or imagined issues. This new situation would be uncomfortable, at least at first, particularly if the teacher group included very many of those cheerful, smiling types that thought, "Lovely day isn't it?" was more than a rhetorical question. Not that I couldn't smile. It's just that if I thought I had to smile, smiles became a burden. *On the plus side*, I told myself, *there would be no more fires to build and floors to sweep.* If I was taken in at Wolffton, the distance to school would decrease from five miles to five blocks, walkable in bad weather. The money would be better; local teachers had a pension plan. And maybe, just maybe, I would find a friend or two among my colleagues. That is, if I wasn't simply dismissed for lack of a diploma.

Assuming that the proposed consolidation would take in the school where I taught, I decided to take my worries to the school board. I asked for a private meeting with the Wolffton board president and got it.

"Consolidation is a ways off, Mrs. Morgan," Todd Schmidt said. He was a board member of some tenure, what some referred to as a "gentleman farmer" or "outsider." There were a number of these landowners around Wolffton—they were younger, earned their living somewhere else and farmed for the love of it, or not at all. Some said that if it wasn't for these folks, consolidation would never have come up in the first place.

"I'm concerned about my place in the district," I told him. "I will have my degree soon and am an active student at Michigan State, but I've heard that might not be good enough."

Todd Schmidt shrugged. "Such details haven't been worked out, that's all I can tell you. If you want my advice, just keep studying and adding credits toward that degree." He paused, before asking, "I'm curious, Mrs. Morgan. Where do you see yourself in a consolidated school district? What are your strengths?"

It sounded as if I were being interviewed. I quickly gathered my thoughts to find an "interview" response.

"My teaching strength is reading. I consider reading the most essential skill and have an enthusiasm for words and books. Of course, I can teach math and science, geography and history too, but reading means most. So I would say that my place would be in those vital grades where reading is emphasized and students are inspired to learn. Elementary grades three to six, I would say, but my personal conviction is that if a student can't read well by the end of fifth grade, he will never gain proficiency."

Mr. Schmidt nodded. "I agree with you there. As an aside, I've reviewed records of country and in-town elementary students and couldn't help but notice that country students tended to surpass in classes where reading is key. Your students are no exception."

So he had reviewed my students' records before this meeting. Well, it seemed I was being taken more seriously than I thought I might be.

A few more exchanges and the interview ended. I felt encouraged, glad that I had sought the meeting. Time would tell, and I could almost hear the clock ticking. A voice in my head said, *One more year.*

The following year came soon enough and with it a ballot vote on school consolidation. "For" and "Against" signs bloomed on town lawns like ungainly flowers. Meetings were held, administrators worried, teachers fretted, and landowners speculated about tax bills. The vote passed, effective with the upcoming school year. I would be two credits short of my degree.

Every day I received telephone calls from someone or other… other teachers, parents from my school district, even a newspaper seeking comment. Now teachers were seeking interviews and reassurance. Contracts would be offered, they were told, just be patience. I was patient. I kept my thoughts to myself, continued my summer studies and waited. I was holding my breath, it seemed, but that sounds ridiculous now. No one holds their breath for an entire summer.

Then came the phone call asking that I meet with school officials. There were a dozen people waiting outside the closed conference room door when I arrived. Some were teachers I knew, others were not. No one was in a talkative mood as we watched one person exit and another enter the room behind that closed door. Sometimes the one leaving was smiling, sometimes not, but all averted their eyes from those of us still awaiting our fate.

"Amelia Morgan."

I followed the tired looking woman into the conference room where six men sat behind a table. The woman closed the door and sat at the end of the table by her notes and pens. There was a chair to her left, and I took it, facing those unsmiling faces across the table.

I recognized Todd Schmidt and he nodded as I caught his eye. The superintendent introduced himself as John Carpenter, a name I didn't know and sailed the names of the others over my head. I waited for the axe to fall.

"Mrs. Morgan," said the superintendent, "We have reviewed your credentials. We are looking for degreed teachers…"

My heart sank.

"…but we can see that you've been diligent in pursuing your degree and lack only two credits. Your teaching record is unblemished, and the board is prepared to offer you a contract."

I was stunned, relieved, speechless. Finally, I said, "Thank you."

Then I recovered and quickly added, "What are the details of the contract?"

"Three years, fifth grade, no more than forty students, standard entry salary, usual health and pension benefits. In your case, a proviso that you will attain your college degree during the term of the contract."

The woman slid an envelope across the table toward me.

"Your contract," said Mr. Carpenter. "We need to know within twenty-four hours if you accept. Return the signed contract to Miss Travis." He nodded toward her. "She'll be here all day tomorrow."

"Thank you, Mr. Carpenter," I said, "And I can tell you now that I accept. I appreciate your confidence in me and will do my best not to disappoint you and the board."

With contract in hand, I leaned across the table and shook hands with everyone, speaking each man's name as it was written on his place card. I needed to remember these names, these faces.

There were still a half-dozen people waiting in the ante-room when I left. I was one of those who smiled a little, averting her eyes from the worried others.

Chapter Eleven

Less than six months passed before Sarah brought her suitcase and sewing machine back home, having decided that Port Austin was not her place. What she thought was another cozy small town turned out to be a tourist/military town that swarmed with wealthy and haughty down-staters in summer and was roiled year-round by four hundred airmen from the nearby base.

Some young women might have liked streets filled with so many uniformed young men but not Sarah. She likened their presence to the carnivals that enlivened county fairs: colorful, tempting and temporary. Besides, she said, there were too many bars with no-coin-return pay telephones. Too often, a payphone user, usually not quite sober, would change his mind midstream and want his money back from a machine that didn't give refunds.

"Too many airmen coming to the office," Sarah said, shaking her head. "Filling out paperwork to get small change, smiling, and making eyes, looking foolish."

I laughed. When had Sarah, still a teenager, become such a cynic? Wasn't there anything she liked about Port Austin?

"Oh, yes," she told me, "Lake Huron. Storm waves as tall as a barn crashing over the pier onto the beach. The way ice piles up on shore in great slippery stacks and seeing the pier become a giant icicle.

"But you can't make a life out of water and ice," she added. "At least I can't."

Cole told Sarah she couldn't stay more than a few days, that her parents' responsibility for her was finished, and she answered, with a toss of her head, that she knew that. She had plans.

And so it was that Sarah found work as a telephone operator in the next county. She shared an apartment with a former schoolmate and, in no time at all, was married to a co-worker a few years older, someone who appeared quiet and steady. No carnival type here, I mused. Quite the contrary. Emmett was bland, maybe too bland. Sarah would run right over him. But that wasn't for me to say.

Catherine, still miles away, was a mother now, and I was grandma. Inevitable, I supposed, that Sarah would follow, Joseph would marry Barbara, and I would eventually be grandma again and again.

Joseph was working with Cole every day now. If they weren't on some road project, they were on the road peddling Indian "relics." Cole boasted that he made as much money on his stones as he did from road building. Money that was his, of course. "Taxable income," my conscience whispered. One more time I thanked my lucky stars that, when I had returned to teaching those few years ago, I had filed my tax return separately from Cole's. That first year, I just went ahead and filed, and when he asked if I was going to do his and our tax return, I said I had already done mine.

Cole was taken aback. "Why didn't you say something, Amy? I could've got my paperwork sooner." He paused, mulling, I suppose, my real reasons. His eyes narrowed.

"You didn't claim Joseph and Emily as your dependents, did you?" I shook my head, no. "Then why do this? What you got up your sleeve?" His face reddened.

I took a deep breath. First, I knew that if there was a refund on any joint tax return, Cole would keep it. As head of the house, he would insist the money was his. Insisting otherwise would do no good and would be apt to bring retaliation, probably some edict that he would pay less for groceries, or utilities, anything to compensate him for his "loss." So I gave him my second reason.

"Cole, it's your side business. You say you make money with your stones but you never show it on your tax form. I worry."

"About what, Amy? Uncle Sam peering in the window, checking the shed? It's a hobby, that's all. None of the government's damn business.

"What do you know, anyway? You suddenly a tax expert? You're just a teacher, remember that. And a timid rabbit of a teacher, at that."

What I did know was that I had already filed my tax return and that the refund soon to come would be mine. And when School Superintendent Carpenter had referred to my "unblemished record," I knew my decision had been the right one. When the day came that Cole was called out on his dealings, he would stand alone.

Joseph told me that Barbara was pregnant and the two of them were getting married. How would he tell his father? His fear was that Cole would be angry and fire him on the spot. I urged Joseph to pick a cool moment, maybe after supper, to announce the news.

"Married." Cole rolled the word off his tongue. "Married. Well, why not? You're a man now, going to be daddy. It's the right thing to do, Joseph. It's the only thing to do."

There was just no predicting Cole's reactions. Joseph was relieved, and so was I. For reasons unknown, we had avoided an expected explosion. Cole was there for the ceremony, as Emily and I were. There were smiles all around, although it was apparent that Barbara's mother wasn't too pleased.

Joseph packed up his clothes, tools, and other belongings and drove them to the apartment he and Barbara had found nearby.

With Joseph gone, the house seemed emptier than ever. Most of the time it was just Emily and me and, of course, the added pleasure of Emily's friends.

On a weekend soon after, Father Morgan came to the house looking for Cole. Mother Morgan had been taken ill, he said, and Alice had taken her to Sparrow hospital.

"She's just not herself," he told me. "She won't eat and just talks nonsense or seems like she can't hear what's said to her."

I could see he was distressed. Father Morgan had always rejected "horspitals," as he called them, believing that once you were in the hospital, you were as good as dead.

"Cole. Where's Cole? He ought to go see his mother before it's too late."

I told him Cole had gone south, to Florida maybe. I wasn't sure myself and hadn't asked. I told Father Morgan that Cole said he would be gone a week or two, but I didn't know exactly where he was or how to get in touch with him.

Father Morgan turned to go, his shoulders sagging.

"Judas Priest," he said, more to himself than to me. "Goldurn dadblamed Cole never around when he should be."

Two days later, Cole came home. He said he cut his trip short and drove straight through because "something" told him to come home.

"What happened?" he demanded, "What happened while I was gone?"

"Your mother," I told him, "Your mother died yesterday."

He slammed out of the house, and I heard his car roaring up the hill to the Morgan farm.

Cole was one of his mother's pallbearers, along with his brother Perry, Alice's husband Ted, and some cousins on the Morgan side. Mother Morgan had said many times that she wanted no strangers touching her or carrying her box. So if she didn't get the first part of that wish, she at least got the last.

It was hard for Cole and he looked for someone to blame. Probably his father, who hadn't got help soon enough, or the hospital which was probably negligent, or Alice, who hadn't driven fast enough taking her mother to the hospital.

The doctors said the main cause of death was malnutrition. I remembered the many times Mother Morgan had made a meal for herself of tea and crackers. The best food, she said, had to be saved for Father Morgan. He worked harder and needed it more.

It was hard to believe that Mother Morgan had starved herself to death right before our eyes. Cole pondered the idea awhile and quieted down. Maybe he concluded, as I did, that if blame was to be doled out, there was plenty to go around.

The next weekend Cole was gone again and life resumed its usual patterns.

Chapter Twelve

Elvis was singing *Don't be Cruel* while Emily and her friends laughed and talked in the living room. Cole was gone, and I was already in bed when Emily came home after the basketball game, friends in tow. I heard her pull my bedroom door closed to block the sound. She needn't have. I actually enjoyed these little get-togethers, liked hearing the music, the laughter, or, as Mother Morgan would have put it had she still been with us, their "carryings on."

I heard the furniture being pushed back and knew the area carpet would be rolled up next. The refrigerator door opened and closed, opened and closed, and I knew the pop that was cooling there would be gone in the morning. Next the sound of someone opening and closing the cookie jar. That, too, would be empty tomorrow.

Another Elvis song, background for the young folks' talk and dance. The record player Emily was using was one Cole had brought home, a little suitcase with carrying handle and stashed electric cord. The machine played one thirty-three vinyl record at a time and was seldom used until Elvis…Emily, her friends and me too were all Elvis fans.

Elvis was more affordable on 45's, so I had bought an adaptor for the player that let our gradually growing stack of Elvis singles play in sequence. It was a genius kind of thing and made me think of the juke boxes where, for a nickel and the touch of a button, you could hear your favorite song, "untouched by human hands" as the saying goes.

Sometimes I put on my housecoat and joined these parties, sometimes not. I didn't want to spoil Emily's fun, but if the doings got too noisy, or if the party went on too long, I would insert myself. The music would be turned down, apologies would be made, and I would ask if anyone wanted cocoa to end the evening. One of the boys called me MaMor and the name stuck. Soon they all called me MaMor and that was fine with me.

This night I listened awhile from the bedroom, finally dozing off to a muffled version of *Hound Dog.*

The next morning the room was back to normal, rug in place, all furniture back on spot. This was Emily's and my agreement: Have fun, dance, eat whatever you find, but don't leave a mess. She and her friends always complied.

I picked up the morning paper from the porch and checked the list of new record releases. No new Elvis singles today. If there had been, Emily and I would be off to Lansing to the only record shop within twenty miles. After the first foray, when we seeded our collection with two or three records, our Lansing trips could be tallied by counting our Elvis records.

Elvis was going to appear on the *The Ed Sullivan Show.* This was a television show I watched regularly when Cole was gone. He wasn't as fond as I of the program, preferring the news or shows with more action. But Cole wouldn't be home until late Sunday, and Emily and I made plans for a big evening together watching Elvis.

All day we talked about it, while we did our ordinary weekend tasks, cleaned up the kitchen, and popped corn.

Just as we settled ourselves in front of the television with our bowls of popcorn and bottles of Pepsi, I heard a car pull into the driveway. It was Cole, not expected until hours later. *The Ed Sullivan Show* was about to begin when Cole came into the living room, saw us, and asked what we were watching. He said there was a boxing match on another channel that he wanted to watch.

I looked at Emily and the expression on her face said it all. There was little doubt in her mind that we would be watching boxing. Before Cole could get to the TV to change channels, I stood up.

"We're watching Ed Sullivan," I said. "Elvis is going to be on, and we've waited all day."

Cole looked surprised. "Elvis? That pipsqueak of a singer?"

Emily looked miserable.

"Yes, Cole, Elvis Presley. Here, have some popcorn and watch it with us."

As soon as Cole had entered the room, Emily had moved from his chair to a new perch. Now Cole took my offered bowl of popcorn and, without a word, sat. I sat too.

When Elvis finally came on and we listened to him sing *Love Me Tender, Don't Be Cruel,* and others, Emily and I were captivated.

After the performance was over, I said to Cole, "Such a sweet boy, Elvis. Don't you think so?"

"Pipsqueak," Cole said, and switched channels.

Emily and I took the empty bowls and Pepsi bottles to the kitchen.

"How'd you do that?" she whispered.

"What?" I said, widening my eyes.

She smiled and so did I as we stifled our laughter. Say no more. We both knew a miracle when we saw one.

Chapter Thirteen

The telephone rang again, the third time this night. I was tempted not to answer. Cole had already left for the week end and Emily was out with friends. But, me, I just couldn't let it ring so I answered.

"Is Cole there?" Another female voice, one I hadn't heard before. The previous two had been unfamiliar, too, and I guessed that Cole was expanding his stable. I hung up without responding.

So he was bored with Lou after all these years. Two-timing me, two-timing Lou, likely two-timing them all. Now in his mid-forties, Cole was still a good-looking man, in some ways more handsome than when he was younger. I had hoped he would get over his chasing ways, exhaust whatever dream he was seeking. *Amy*, I told myself, as the phone rang again, *it isn't going to happen.*

I heard a car pull into the driveway. It was Cole and I could tell he was angry by the sound of the car door slamming. He stormed into the kitchen.

"Where's Emily?"

"Out with her friends. Probably driving around or at someone's house. Is something wrong?"

"You might say that. I was just driving through town, had to stop at the light. There was a bunch of kids hanging around on the corner. I saw one of them look my way. Then they were all staring, and I thought I saw Emily, pretty sure it was Emily. When the light changed and I pulled away, someone in that bunch gave me the finger. Damn kids! Giving me the finger! Emily's friends, no doubt."

"Were you alone?"

"So what if I wasn't? Lou was with me and so upset I took her home and left her off, still blubbering. Emily better explain herself."

Cole dropped into his chair in front of the TV, then got up and popped himself a kettle of popcorn. So he was planning to stay.

Emily's curfew was eleven, and I prayed she would be home on time. Surprisingly, she burst in about ten o'clock, saying she needed a sweater. Several of her friends were in the car outside, waiting.

By now, Cole had taken a magazine and moved to the bedroom where he was reading and finishing the remains of his popcorn.

"Emily, come in here." Hearing the tone of Cole's voice, Emily gave me a questioning glance. I just shook my head and she went into the bedroom. I followed and stood at the door, watching.

"Yes, Daddy?"

"Remember that ring I gave you on your birthday? Well, I've decided I want it back."

Emily started to say something but didn't. She looked from Cole to me, and then at her hand which wore the gold ring with its small stone. Without a word, she removed the ring and handed it toward Cole.

Maybe he expected her to plead. Maybe he expected her to cry. Whatever he expected, compliance was not it. Clearly infuriated, he struck the ring from her fingers, threw back the bed cover and, with a sound that was half yell, half growl, lunged toward Emily. I felt the hairs on my neck rising.

"Run, Emily, run!" I pushed her hard behind me and stayed in the doorway. I could hear the door slam and her friend's car leave the driveway with squealing tires.

Cole, wearing only his boxers, reached for his trousers.

"She'll not get away with that. No one walks away from me when I'm talking." *Blood in his eye*, my mind whispered. *Blood in his eye.*

I grabbed my purse and headed for my own car. I had barely backed into the street and started out when I heard Cole's car behind me. I drove faster. Where to go? Who would be up this time of night? The only one I could think of was Cole's sister, Alice. Her place was about two miles away. She would be up, probably reading or sewing. As I drove, I worried that Cole would speed up and pass on the two-lane road, maybe force me into the ditch. I needn't have worried, he simply followed, close, and we pulled into Alice's driveway together.

"Where's Emily?" he shouted. "I thought Emily was with you."

I said nothing and hurried to the door. One knock and Alice was there. She looked surprised...once to see me, and twice to see Cole. That was the sum-total of her reaction as she invited us in. She had coffee and cookies and we ate them at the kitchen table. No questions, no words about our late arrival or the reasons behind the visit. Finally, Cole left and, after a few minutes, so did I. Cole's outburst had run its course and I went home. Cole was asleep, his rage drained as fast as it had arisen.

Emily didn't come home until morning. Cole was still asleep when she walked in, followed by the young man who had driven her home. She told me she had slept on the couch at his house and that his mother had made her breakfast.

"What was Daddy so angry about?" she asked. "Is he still mad?"

"I think it was about some young people disrespecting him downtown," I told her. "He thought one of them was you. He's probably forgotten it by now. Let's just not talk about it."

Emily and the boy exchanged a look that told me Cole had not been mistaken.

"If you're okay," the boy said, "I'll get back home. I still have chores to do."

"Thanks," Emily said, and waved as he quietly backed from the driveway. No squealing tires this time.

When Cole awoke ready for breakfast, it was as if nothing had happened. As for the ring, I found it when I was tidying up the bedroom and put it in my jewelry box. If Cole asked, I would produce it. If not, it would rest there for another time.

The details of this episode haunted my thoughts and my dreams, casting a more ominous light on the many earlier clashes between Cole, Catherine, Sarah, and Joseph.

It looked to be Emily's turn. Fear sat in my stomach, roiling and burning like an indigestible meal.

I told myself that when the time was right, I would know what to do. When the time was right, I would be shown the way. For now, I should continue, one day at a time, with an eye to the sky and my own index finger held politely to the wind.

Chapter Fourteen

Barbara telephoned to say that Joseph had been admitted to the hospital. When she drove him to the Emergency room at Sparrow, he was bleeding from the bowel. "Not just spotting," she said, by way of explanation, "A river." She began to cry.

"I'll be right there," I told her.

Joseph was pale and in pain when I saw him. He was connected to various paraphernalia and was getting a blood transfusion.

"It just kept getting worse," Joseph said. "I told them I had been losing blood for a while, months even, and that my doctor had given me hemorrhoid medicine. I almost passed out at work yesterday and Dad was really ticked."

"Do they know what's wrong?"

"Not really. They just said I needed blood. They used the word 'colitis'."

"Where are the boys?" I asked Barbara. There were two babies now, the youngest only two months old.

"Mom's taking care of them. She was at the house anyway, and when Joseph nearly passed out and wasn't making much sense, she told me to bring him here. I'm just glad she was there."

She was there many days after that too, as Joseph's hospitalization extended into weeks, then months. Finally, when his condition didn't improve, Joseph said that the doctor told him it was time for surgery. "You can't keep living on other people's blood," the doctor said. "You are not healing, and we need to try surgery." By this time, Joseph had bled out more than forty pints of transfused blood.

Joseph's weight plummeted. His six-foot, 190 pound frame had diminished by a third and, as his weight dropped, so did his strength.

It was hoped that the surgery, besides stopping bleeding, would help him gain back some weight. As it was, he ate little and intravenous feedings seemed ineffective. So surgery was done to remove his diseased colon. The surgeon said it was riddled with lesions, the worst case of ulcerative colitis he had seen. Now Joseph had an colostomy.

Cole rarely came to the hospital. He was angry; angry with me, angry with Joseph, angry with Frank, his boss at work. Cole and Frank had clashed again a few days before Joseph was hospitalized, and Cole couldn't get it out of his mind. Over and over, for months now, he relived that encounter.

"Can you believe that jackass keeps on telling me how to run my crew? Plucking that one-string guitar of his that says I'm too hard on Joseph? Saying can't you see he's not feeling well? Well, I told him just mind your own damn business. He's my son and he's been slacking lately, taking time to sit when he should be standing, just not keeping up. Not on my crew, not on my job."

I was tired of hearing his rant, had heard one version or another too many times before.

"Joseph's very sick, Cole. Surely you can see that. Maybe Frank just saw his sickness before you did."

He swung around to face me. "Oh yes, Amy, you know all about it. You and Frank know, even when your fancy doctors don't. You both want to blame me. Well, go ahead, if it makes you feel better. But you, you always taking Joseph's side, babying him.

I'll tell you what made him sick. You and your goddamn mother love. So don't talk to me about it."

He pushed past me and out the door. I heard the familiar sound of his car spinning gravel as he backed it to the road.

I pulled a chair back from the dining room table and sat. There was this hollow ringing inside my head and my ears were filled with the sound of my heart beating, thumping against my ribs.

I screamed until it seemed that the air in my empty house was ringing with sound. "Damn you, Cole, damn you, damn you." I sobbed, wishing Cole gone, wishing him dead, wishing him burnt in hell. I thought of killing him myself.

"Now, Amy, you'll do no such thing." The voice in my head was Pa's, calm and firm as always. *"Get ahold of yourself. Faith and prayer, faith and prayer."*

I waited for more words that didn't come, realized I was holding my breath, and exhaled. I reminded myself that there were student papers to correct, studying to be done for my college finals. That could wait. I needed to drive to the hospital to see Joseph.

In spite of the surgery, Joseph continued to lose weight. Barbara telephoned to say that he was being moved from the main hospital to The Annex, a separate building two or three blocks distant from the main hospital. When I walked into The Annex where four or five people sat in a large waiting room, the starkness of the place stopped me in my tracks. I looked around at the chalky pastel walls and bare windows.

"What is this place?" I said aloud. A woman stopped thumbing her magazine and looked at me. "It's modern medicine's version of death row," she said, before turning back to her magazine. "They don't kill you here. They just wait."

A death sentence. Joseph was going to die. I would have dropped to my knees there in the waiting room had I not been caught by another waiting visitor. He held my arm firmly, steadying me before returning to his seat. Neither of us spoke and I continued to the desk where I signed in before walking those cheerless halls to the cubicle where Joseph lay.

Just before Joseph was moved, Barbara had been reminded that Joseph's hospital stay was nearing the 120 days covered by his insurance. Arrangements needed to be made. Someone had to promise to pay and the doctors had given up.

I had no idea where such money would come from or what to do next and while I was thinking about it, Barbara's mother, who was visiting when I walked in, spoke up. "If the family is going to have to pay for this," she said, "Joe should be someplace where they know what they're doing. Obviously that's not here…he's only gotten worse in four months."

"But where?" I asked. "Who'll take him with no insurance?"

"Henry Ford hospital in Detroit. It's the best hospital I know of. I've been there myself and found out that if Joseph comes in through emergency, they won't refuse him."

An ambulance was the only way Joseph could be moved and that cost had to be paid in advance. I asked Cole for the money. He said he'd pay half. I paid the rest and Joseph was moved to Henry Ford hospital on the 121st day of his hospitalization in Lansing. Barbara and I followed the ambulance in my car, keeping pace so as not to get lost. Freeways had replaced the more familiar Grand River Avenue route, and this was my first plunge into the Lodge, a six-lane ditch that took cars and trucks into the heart of Detroit. Barbara, usually talkative, said little. She sensed, correctly, how intensely I was focused on driving.

"Keep an eye on the ambulance," I told her. "Say something when you think it's going to turn." Even when cars got between us and the ambulance, we could see its height and lights. That's what kept us on track to the Grand Boulevard exit and hospital emergency entrance.

The hospital was huge, six, no probably eight stories tall, brick upon brick. There were several ambulances already there, some with lights flashing. I could see parking lots spreading away from the buildings, so expansive that the entire downtown of Wolffton could have been relocated there, with room to spare.

I pulled in close to the emergency door, and Barbara and I walked in to face the paperwork together. When they told Barbara "an adult" would have to sign Joseph in, she laughed out loud. She was his wife and the mother of two but a year short of her twenty-first birthday. I signed. While Joseph was being examined, we waited in this little cubicle with pale green walls. Barbara chattered nervously, as was her style. I barely listened, waiting, waiting, waiting…

Finally a young man who looked about Joseph's age opened the door. He wore a white coat, serious expression and a name tag that said "Doctor".

"Mrs. Morgan?" He never blinked when we both responded "yes."

"I'm Doctor Phillips. We've taken a look at Joseph, and there's some things you should know. Obviously he's seriously ill. He weighs eighty-nine pounds and odds of his survival are pretty low, about 40 percent. Here at Ford we'll do everything we can for him, and I must say that's considerable. We have a Dr. Barron on staff who's an expert in this sort of thing. You'll be meeting with him later. Meanwhile, someone from Administration will talk to you. This is going to be a long, expensive hospitalization. Whatever the outcome, you're going to need help."

"It's the money next," I whispered to Barbara as Dr. Phillips left, envisioning my signature on a document that would mortgage my life to the end. Unlike Cole, who might go half, I would go whole hog. It was Joseph's life on the line, after all. I couldn't believe it when we were told, not how much to pay, but how to apply for assistance to cover costs. Barbara was also given a phone number to call for help with rent and living expenses.

Even though the news on Joseph's health was dire, I felt encouraged. There was something about this place, something about the people that was encouraging. I just knew these people would do their absolute best. Their confidence was contagious.

We waited until Joseph was in his room and made a brief visit. He was tired from the grueling day but tried to smile when he saw us. Apparently Joseph was encouraged too. There had been no smiles at Lansing for months.

The sun was going down when we left, found the freeway entrance, and headed home. I had driven the Lodge and survived. Next time would be easier—I would get used to the freeway traffic, horn-blowing and general madness of these city drivers with their hair streaming out car windows. In fact, after a half-dozen or so of these high-speed excursions, weekly trips would become almost routine.

Chapter Fifteen

Joseph was under the care of several doctors and one of them was Dr. Barron. He told us, to put it plainly, that Joseph was starving to death, his system unable to assimilate nourishment. He had seen cases like this before and had invented a feeding machine to overcome the deficiency.

"It's new," he said. "Joseph will be our second patient to use the pump." Even though the first patient hadn't survived, Dr. Barron was confident. "He's too young for us to just give up. We won't quit as long as he's breathing."

The machine was a pump and container filled with high-calorie slush, something like a milkshake, that was pumped through a nasal tube into the stomach. It ran night and day, slow or fast, sometimes quiet for a time for reasons known only to Dr. Barron.

More than a month went by. Joseph looked thinner and more haggard, reminding me of LIFE magazine photos of prisoners in World War II concentration camps. My heart twisted to see him this way, to think this way, and I prayed, implored, "Don't take my son, don't take my Joseph."

Then the day came when Dr. Barron told Barbara that Joseph had gained weight. From a low of seventy-four pounds his weight had begun to climb. Photos of Joseph were taken that day by the hospital staff and Dr. Barron said that these and earlier photos—and more to come—would be used as teaching tools. "So," he said, looking at Joseph over the top of his glasses, "You will become a famous case, maybe save someone else's life too. Good, right?"

Joseph smiled and nodded. Remembering how Joseph had despised the intrusions of visiting students at Sparrow, I wondered what magic Dr. Barron had worked here.

Summer was in full swing, and it seemed odd not to be attending classes. I had completed my studies at Michigan State, passed exams and earned my degree. My diploma, and a copy for the school board come fall, were stashed in my dresser, away from Cole's eyes. I feared it would be just one more reason for a rant against teaching, against me, and perhaps end up with my diploma torn to shreds.

Catherine phoned, saying that she and Sarah would stop by for a visit. What a surprise when they showed up with cards and a cake for my graduation. Emily was in on it too, and we all sat around visiting and eating cake.

"Not everyone has a mother who graduates from college when she's fifty plus," Catherine said. "Congratulations, Mother. We're so proud of you." For a few hours, thoughts of Joseph were not at the forefront.

About this time, a neighbor knocked on my door. She was from a local women's club that had come up with the idea of a money-raising benefit for Joseph. I was somewhat taken aback—it had never occurred to me that the townspeople knew, or cared about Joseph's troubles. Some of my friends at school and around the neighborhood asked about him now and then but perhaps I was too wrapped up in my own worry and dread to imagine any interest beyond that.

I listened to her ideas—a dance, canisters, raffles, bake sales, car washes–such an assortment of generous ideas, each of them requiring the efforts of many people.

Cole wouldn't like it. It would sound too much like charity to him. *But this isn't about him,* I reminded myself. *This is about Joseph.*

"I think you should talk to Barbara," I said. "It's a good, generous idea. But Joseph is married now, and I shouldn't be the one to say. I'll give you her phone number."

We left it at that.

The benefit idea was like a snowball rolling downhill. Signs were up all over town. Canisters with Joseph's graduation picture were everywhere–the grocery, bank, drug store, even the bar. Car washes were held on several Saturdays, with high schoolers cheerfully taking on the task. A reporter showed up to take pictures and do interviews that ended up on the pages of the Lansing State Journal.

I was floored by such an outpouring. Cole said little, one way or the other. He was still angry and agitated and came home less and less. Road jobs across the state kept him on the road, as always, but now he hauled his little trailer everywhere, staying nights even when he might have driven home. When he did show up, Cole was tight-faced and pre-occupied and we avoided talking about certain subjects, especially Joseph and Emily.

I knew that Joseph's illness tormented Cole and that his inability to talk about it added to the torture but there was nothing I could do. This was his problem, not mine, and I might not have helped him even if I could. I was angry too. To make things worse, his disapproval rating of Emily had intensified since the ring incident, and I didn't know why. I wasn't about to risk open warfare by asking.

The big event of the benefit drive was a dance at the Community Hall downtown. The hall was a focal point of the town, its largest meeting place until the new school gymnasium was built a few years earlier. Until then, basketball games were played there, plays were performed on its stage, and flowers and quilts were exhibited. Any event was made more important by happening in the hall.

Sarah was quick to enlist her husband's musical group to provide music. Emmett played drums alongside a saxophone and fiddle. Sometimes a group member played piano if one was available. Or another friend, an accordionist joined in, and the fiddler called square dances. Despite their number, they called themselves *The Starlight Trio* and, I must admit, provided varied and rousing music during the *Joseph Morgan Benefit Dance.*

The crowd at the Community Hall that night overflowed into the street and the fire department accommodated the crowd by blocking off a large section with saw horses. It seemed the whole town was there, dancing upstairs or visiting the bake sales, games and refreshment window in the basement, where more canisters stood in rows. Someone set up a tape recorder and people lined up to leave a message for Joseph.

Emily seemed to be everywhere, spinning around in her lime green flared skirt, dancing to nearly every tune. Barbara, the center of attention with her two dressed-up boys, stayed long after her mother took the boys home to bed. Cole was nowhere to be seen.

What a morale booster this community outpouring was. A sizeable amount of money was raised over the several weeks the drive continued, but it wasn't the money that made the difference, it was the people coming together in this way.

Joseph had seemed only slightly interested when we mentioned the town's benefit drive. Now, hearing the recorded voices of friends, neighbors, former schoolmates, and people whose names he didn't even know, Joseph rallied. The messages were happy, supportive, silly, uplifting, joking. Not a gloomy sentence among them. Joseph laughed and played the tape over and over, energized by all these voices. I hadn't seen this sparkle in his eyes for months.

Emily said later that she thought the recording was the turning point in Joseph's recovery. Maybe so, but I believe that the church's prayer vigil, the concentrated power of their earnest prayers beamed in Joseph's direction, was key. Either way, it was clear that Joseph was getting better.

Five months after Joseph began his stay at Henry Ford hospital, he was discharged. More surgery had been done to close his colostomy and replace it with something they called a "pull-through" that restored his body to normal function. He walked carefully, like an old man, but he was walking. That he could walk at all was a small miracle. I remembered painfully that he couldn't stand without help just weeks before. Now he weighed a thin one hundred and twenty pounds but no longer had that starved look that was so frightening to see. Dr. Barron was there when Joseph left, giving instructions in his firm, calm voice. "You will do as I say, won't you?" he asked, looking intently over his glasses into Joseph's eyes.

Joseph smiled and nodded, "Yes, I will. I'll do like you say."

So Joseph went home with Barbara to continue his recovery. There were frequent follow-up appointments at Henry Ford, where they charted his progress and took still more photos. It would still be months, even years, before a full recovery, but I was sure that the worst was over.

Thank you, Lord, thank you, Dr. Barron.

PART FOUR

Begin Again

Since the episode between Emily and Cole, that she and I tried to minimize by calling "the great car chase," she pretty much steered clear of Cole to the extent she could. In other words, her social life hinged on Cole's absences, always overshadowed by the fear that he might unexpectedly show up.

Emily was getting ready to graduate high school. Not only that, she was planning to be married soon after graduation. It seemed rather sudden to me, but certainly I remembered about "sudden" and how that worked. Emily had known Aaron during high school since his transfer to town from country school. He was a quiet boy, clean and polite, his personality noticeably honed by a conservative religious upbringing. Mentally, I contrasted his tamped down demeanor and behavior with Emily's happy-go-lucky social ways and wondered whether the arrangement would work. But, as with the others, I felt it was not for me to say and kept my concerns to myself.

After his own graduation a year before Aaron had joined the Air Force. Now he wanted Emily to come to Lincoln, Nebraska. So we planned a small garden wedding at Sarah's home. She and Catherine became wedding planners and began sewing dresses.

Cole and I barely spoke anymore. He was less agitated now that Joseph was out of hospital, but he still carried an edge of animosity that stemmed, I thought, from guilt. He would have denied it, of course, but then, we never discussed it.

I was sitting at the dining room table, reviewing student papers, when I heard a car in the driveway. Cole walked in and headed for the bedroom. I could hear that the car was still running and see from the window that its lights were on. I waited for Cole to come back.

"Find what you want?" I asked, mostly for civil conversation.

"Yeah," Cole said, "A guy at the Pioneer said he was interested in jackknives and I told him I had a few. He's waiting at the bar to take a look." In his hands he held several Case knives in their boxes; others bulged in his jacket pocket.

"You left the car running."

He gave me a look that I read correctly.

"She's in the car, isn't she? You had the nerve to bring Lou here to my home." I pushed my chair back and stood up. "I have a few words for her."

"It's not Lou," he said, grabbing my arm to stop me from leaving the kitchen. "It's no one you have a beef with."

"No one I have a beef with? You have a funny way of looking at things, Cole. I'm sure you would see it differently if it were me coming home with some guy waiting in the car."

"Don't start, Amy. I'm not here ten minutes and you're at me. Any wonder I stay away?" He turned toward the door.

"Wait a minute, Cole," I said and he stopped, looked at me with questioning eyes. I went into the bedroom, retrieved his pillow from the bed, brought it to the kitchen and pushed it into his chest

"Take it," I said, "That's just about all of you that's left here, anyway."

Standing there, hugging the pillow, Cole looked confused, even a little sheepish.

"I...I don't know where I'll sleep tonight," he said. The comment struck me first as outrageous, then as laughable. This was just another bit of the same old malarkey.

"I'm sure you'll think of something," I said, in as cold a tone as I could muster. Without a word, Cole turned and left, still clutching the pillow, leaving the door ajar. I heard his car back slowly from the driveway, into the street and away. I closed the door, locked it and looked at the clock. Almost eleven. Emily would be home soon.

Papers were still strewn across the table. I got a glass of water, sat again at my "desk," picked up a pencil, and burst into tears. I was still teary when Emily came into the house, calling good-byes to her departing friends.

"Your father's gone," I told her. "This time for good."

Emily's smile disappeared and, for a moment, she said nothing. Then she asked, "Are you sure?" I nodded, and we just looked at each other before she turned, said, "Good night," and started upstairs to bed.

The next day I called a lawyer that Sarah recommended. Cole was served divorce papers the following week.

This was not the end of it, of course. Cole showed up one night soon after, just walked in without knocking, and said he was here for his things. In the bedroom, he began pulling clothes from the closet and the dresser and stacking them on the bed. He took a picture off the wall, added it to the pile and turned his attention to the dressers. Atop the low dresser was a photo of Cole, Pa and Connie's husband, Wes. It was a photo I cherished, a reminder, if not of happier times, at least of a time when there was still hope for Cole and me. In the picture, the three handsome men stood close together in the backyard, wearing suits and vests, half- smiling into the camera. Cole held a lighted cigarette in one hand.

Cole picked up the picture, held it a moment and turned it over. He took the photo from its frame. I held my breath.

"You want me gone, you won't want this," he said, and I watched while he tore the photo lengthwise, stripping away his own image from the others. He threw the scrap on the floor and left the rest on the dresser.

I had been hurt worse. If I was going to cry, it would be later. I watched as Cole filled his arms with clothes and walked through the house to his car. There were boxes in the garage and paper bags in the kitchen that he might have used, but I said nothing. I ignored the sock that dropped from his load and went into the living room to read.

"I want that chair too." Cole was back, pointing to the chair we had always referred to as "his" chair. He waited for me to object.

"Take it," I said.

"And the gate-leg, too." He was referring to the walnut dining table that he knew meant a lot to me. I kept quiet on this one, having no intention of letting him take it.

"I'll get them next time," he said, "There's no room in the car."

"Next time, knock," I told him.

"Don't get too uppity, there, Mrs. Morgan," he countered. "This is still my house, and I am still your husband. I'll come here whenever I want until the papers say otherwise. Next time, I'll bring the pickup."

My lawyer served Cole with papers that kept him from entering the house and the court sent him a letter stating the amount he had to pay for Emily's support. I was glad that I was not nearby when he got those notices. I also told my lawyer than any property agreement should specify the walnut gate-leg as mine. I would not bend on this one.

My lawyer urged me to provide names and details of Cole's infidelities. Michigan was not a "no-fault" divorce state then and reasons had to be given. I knew there would be hell to pay if I provided such details and so I declined. The lawyer, grumbling, used the words, "adultery" and "mental cruelty" instead. I got a letter from Cole's lawyer saying that Cole wanted half of everything.

In the midst of all this, a member of Cole's work crew came to my door. Gavin was the father of the worker who had collected Cole's company pickup from the chest hospital all those years earlier.

"Would you like to come in?" Gavin just shook his head and remained on the porch.

"The reason I'm here," he said, shifting his weight from one foot to the other, "Is because of the troubles between you and Cole. He says you want a divorce and that you have no cause, that is, no cause you can prove. He says it's a property argument and he intends to get it all, including this house." He gestured with his hat, in an arc meant to encompass the walls, the roof, the porch where he stood.

"What I'm saying, Mrs. Morgan," he continued, "is that I've worked with Cole a long time. So have my boys. If you need help to prove anything about his behavior, you just let me know. Me and my boys can give you names and places and we will. That's what I came here to say." He put his hat atop his head and turned to leave.

I thanked him and watched as he walked to his truck and drove away. To think that one of Cole's own work crew would stand by me, risk having to face up to Cole on the job…well, it was dumbfounding. Here, in front of my eyes, was one more example of community support. I never expected it and, until Joseph, never knew such a thing existed. One more thing to be thankful for.

Chapter Two

Emily's class had already marched into the gymnasium for graduation ceremonies when Cole walked in. He had a woman with
him, and I wondered if it was Lou. The two of them sat near the
back and, even though I itched for a better look, I resisted craning
my neck to look backward from my seat nearer the front.

One by one, students were called forward to receive their
diplomas. Alice's daughter, Cherie, stepped forward to accept
hers. Cherie was born only months before Emily and the two
were fast friends. Seeing her, I remembered Alice's offer to raise
Emily, and was grateful I hadn't taken her up on it. Emily had
added so much joy to hundreds of hard days. Hers was the smile
and spark that kept me going. Catherine had chided me once for
spoiling Emily, saying I catered to her, demanded little from her
and treated her like something special. Well, the truth was that
Emily was special. She made my life livable and I tried not to
think of her wedding, only months away.

Emily's name was called and she accepted her paper and took
her place among the other students standing at the back of the
stage. One of the students nudged her, whispered something, and
Emily glanced briefly toward the back of the hall. Someone had
spotted her father and passed the word. I saw a number of the

students look toward Emily with concern and smiled to myself. Emily was not alone here.

Afterward, Emily joined me where I sat, soon followed by a half-dozen of her gowned classmates, all laughing and, yes, protective. Cole was waiting in the entrance hall when we walked out. He never spoke to Emily, just stood there, talking to others he knew and greeting Cherie with his great laugh. Loudly enough for Emily to hear, he said to Cherie, "I had to come see you graduate tonight. My sister's girl. That's the reason I'm here."

Emily, who had been waiting beside me for the right moment to speak to her father, turned away. She was immediately encased in a cloud of black-gowned graduates who spirited her away down the hall, laughing and talking the whole time. I would see her later at home.

Now I turned to take a look at Cole and the woman with him. I wanted to see how confident Lou looked here in my world, my school environment. She was standing to Cole's right, her face partly hidden. I stared until she looked up, straight into my eyes, and smiled.

It wasn't Lou at all. It was Velna, a woman I knew, a near neighbor whose daughter was only slightly younger than Emily. To say I was surprised was to put it mildly. Vel, as she liked to be called, was a fixture at the gas station and garage her husband owned downtown. The two of them had worked the business together until his death—Vel had pumped gas for my Ford many times. She was at the station every day in jeans and some kind of dark or plaid shirt, her lean figure and short bobbed hair not much different than the young men who worked in the garage. Even when pumping gasoline, her hand most likely held a cigarette, lit and smoking, whether smoked or not. At a distance, she might have been mistaken for a weathered movie cowboy.

I had heard a rumor that Velna was man-hunting now that she was widowed and that she had her eye on Cole. Come to think of it, Cole was the one who told me. Judging by the evidence before my eyes, he must have been drawn into the hunt.

Vel's eyes were still on me. Without smiling, I nodded and turned away, wanting neither to be uncivil nor cordial. After all, Cole was on his own these days and nights, if not yet single. He never looked my way and that was fine with me. He knew I was there.

At home, Emily breezed in with a carload of friends, dropping by to cast off her cap and gown before going to a party. Her friends left their gowns as well and called their goodbyes as they poured out the door, leaving the house empty and quiet. There was nothing on TV worth watching and, after a while, I went to bed, thinking about Emily's upcoming wedding and the kind of day it would be.

If you wanted someone to plan your party, Sarah was the one. There was no doubt that the day's events would be orderly, timely, and all-inclusive. Handwritten invitations were distributed, refreshments were planned and a local minister agreed to perform the ceremony. No detail would be overlooked—you could count on Sarah for that. Barbara would be matron of honor and an Air Force buddy of Aaron's was coming from Lincoln to serve as best man.

Sarah's and Emmett's house was not very large and the twenty or so guests looked like a big crowd. Vows were exchanged in front of the fireplace and the after-party continued on the large country lawn. A two-tiered cake had been baked the day before in Sarah's oven and prettily decorated by Cherie. Catherine's and Sarah's daughters posed and spun in identical filmy blue dresses Catherine had made, and Emily looked every bit the bride in the linen and lace ensemble Sarah had put together. Joseph, rail thin but cheerful, was there to give his sister away. Overall, the event made a pretty summer picture and we all cherished the photos Emmett took that day.

Cole was not part of it. No handwritten invitation had been sent his way. After the graduation snub, we all supported Emily's tearful decision to exclude him.

Aaron's leave from Lincoln Air Force Base would end in a few days. Emily and Aaron packed their few belongings into his car and they were gone. I could only imagine their destination, a one-room apartment, bath down the hall that Aaron had rented ahead of time.

I wandered through the house, picking up remnants of Emily's presence until the emptiness of the rooms seemed overwhelming. I thought of Ma, how she must have felt when the last chick had flown. She had told me, more than once, that hard work was the remedy for life's rough moments. In my memory I could almost see her, down on her hands and knees, brush in hand, vigorously scrubbing the kitchen floor. I got my bucket and mop and set to work. The exercise didn't help my blue mood much, but at least the floor was clean.

Chapter Three

Sarah offered to go to court with me for the divorce hearing. She must have sensed my nervousness, or maybe was just being protective. At any rate, I was grateful for the offer. She drove. Sarah always drove if she had a choice and I offered to buy lunch afterward.

Truth to tell, I was feeling anxious, worrying about meeting Cole face-to-face. Earlier hearings had disabused Cole of any ideas he might have had about grabbing the house or my other things. He claimed victory when the court said I would have to pay him "his share." The amount was modest and seemed fair–I kept my resentment to myself and let Cole crow. Frankly, it was a relief that the agreement precluded a messy court display of Cole's dirty laundry and there would be no need for the testimony Gavin had offered. This final hearing was little more than a formality. Even so, there was no predicting how Cole would react.

Sarah parked on the street, and we walked together toward the stone monolith that was the county courthouse. Its clock tower was still the tallest structure in town, its steps the steepest, its terrazzo floors the shiniest. Like its county sisters across the state, the edifice had been built to impress, appropriating real estate from the center of a fledgling town almost before there was any real center. I was a child when this courthouse was built and first saw it when Cole and I came here together to apply for our marriage license. Now I had returned, but it was not so much fun this time.

We climbed the stone steps to the main floor, then climbed the second flight to the courtroom. Out of breath, I asked Sarah to wait. I didn't want to be huffing and puffing when I faced Cole. Once we were in the courtroom, my lawyer joined us and we sat down to wait for our case to be called. Neither Cole nor his lawyer had arrived.

We went over the papers to be signed. I would sign them, every one, telling myself that the house payoff was a small price to pay for freedom. I had vowed to myself that I would not move out, would not give up the place, and so I would pay. Cole had already removed his chair, his grinders, tumblers, other relic-making tools, and a few other things he claimed just to be ornery. The exchange had been made a month earlier, under the watchful eye of a neighbor I enlisted for the job. The walnut gate-leg stayed.

Cole came into the courtroom laughing, his smiling lawyer at his side. Cole glanced in our direction as if we were strangers and then turned his smiles on strangers as if they were friends. His laugh, warm and hearty, attracted attention and most everyone in the room looked toward him and smiled, and he smiled in return. The Grand Entrance. That was Cole, all over.

When our case was called, it took all of five minutes for the judge to complete the process. "Petition granted."

Sarah and I waited a moment at the witness table. I was hoping Cole would leave first but he was waiting too, and finally Sarah and I began our trek back to the car. Cole followed.

When we were outside, he caught up with us and walked beside me, shortening his stride to match my steps. I could feel Sarah stiffen as we kept walking.

"Are you happy now?" Cole's tone was calm, a little sarcastic.

I stopped, turned toward him.

"Cole, what do you want? Am I supposed to be happy now, after trying for more than thirty years to make that...marriage work? Why ask me now when that question never passed your lips in all those years? Let me put it this way: I have the children and the house. What do you have? Lou?"

Cole smiled and gave a deprecating wave of one hand.

"Not Lou. She's nothing but a fat ass. That's done."

I was speechless. I thought of the irony of it; her two-decade wait because Cole was married and now ditched when he was free.

"Well, good luck, Cole. I wish you well." That's what I said, not wishing to create a scene in front of the biggest building in town. It wasn't necessarily what I meant.

"Come on, Sarah, let's get some lunch."

I opened the car door and got in. Sarah did the same and, before getting in, I heard her say, "'Bye, Dad."

Cole turned and walked away. I reached for the handkerchief in my purse, blew my nose and felt the tears begin pouring down my cheeks. I wept, as quietly as I could, while Sarah waited. She might have said something, but I didn't hear her words.

Sarah started the car and we drove around town for a while, eventually stopping for coffee. Neither of us was hungry nor had much to say. Sarah told a story about my lawyer that was meant to amuse but didn't. We didn't see anyone we knew and that was a blessing.

When Sarah pulled into the drive at home, Joseph's car was ahead of us and he got out to meet us. Of course he knew I was going to court today. Sarah stayed in her car and waved goodbye, wanting to be off on afternoon errands. Joseph waited while I got out of her car.

"How'd it go?" Joseph asked, even before we were in the house.

"It went okay. No surprises, no yelling, nothing like that. Do you want something to eat?"

"Maybe a Pepsi." He helped himself from the refrigerator and we sat at the kitchen table.

"Well, I had a little surprise," Joseph said. "Frank came by the house today."

"Frank? You mean your father's boss?"

"Mine, too. He stopped by to see when I can come back to work."

I gasped. "So soon? You've hardly had time to gain your strength back."

"True, but I'm getting stronger. Frank wanted me to know that my job was waiting. We talked a long time and he told me that if I could only work two hours a day, that would be okay, and when I could work more, the hours would be there. And he said he had a new job for me." Joseph smiled, a rueful kind of smile, but he looked pleased too.

"Frank said when I was ready they would train me to run the automated concrete plant. It's lighter work, no lifting to speak of, a kind of desk job without a desk." He looked at me for my reaction.

"No outside work then? No working with your father?"

Joseph nodded. "Dad won't like it. He'll want me back on his crew. But Mother, I don't think I can do it anymore. Besides, I don't want to do it. Frank's giving me a good chance, and I'm thinking about taking it."

"Take it, Joseph. Tell him you'll take it, just as soon as you're ready. Do you know what I think? I think Frank has his eyes open on your situation and is doing something about it." I reached over and took Joseph's hand.

"It's time you're out from under your father's thumb, Joseph. Your apprenticeship is over. Frank is offering a great opportunity."

"Well, I'm a little nervous about computer stuff. Most I ever operated was an adding machine. But he says that doesn't matter. There is one thing that worries me more…"

He stopped and I waited. Finally, I asked "What?"

"It's my running to the bathroom all the time. Dr. Barron said my gut would settle down, but for now it's so unpredictable and often. So, you'll never believe this, but I said that to Frank. I was embarrassed but I said it anyway."

"What did Frank say?"

Joseph looked at me and grinned. "He said, 'It doesn't matter. We'll rent a porta-john in your name and park it wherever you are. You'll be the only one on the job with a private john.'"

We both laughed then, partly for the humor of Frank's words, but out of relief, too, release of embarrassment, and gratitude.

The tears we both wiped away weren't all from laughter. Frank's gesture was overwhelming. More than that, it was life changing. We both knew that, because of Frank, Joseph's tomorrows would be changed forever for the better.

Chapter Four

The whole tone of my life changed. The house felt huge and hollow. When the telephone rang it was someone I knew, one of the children, perhaps, or a member of the teaching staff. No more calls from floozies tracking Cole. I found I was still listening for Emily's curfew entrance, or for Cole's car in the driveway.

Teaching filled my days, student paperwork most evenings. I still had more time left over than ever before in my life. I filled those hours with thinking and looking at my rooms. They needed painting, wallpapering, something.

I was making house payments, the court-ordered debt to pay off *Cole's share*. I had dreaded going back to the bank after my earlier experience, but Mrs. Wilson had taken ill. She told me on the telephone that she had to give up lending out what she might need herself. So now I visited the bank every month, making payments and acknowledging the manager's practiced smile with a tight smile of my own. I looked forward to the day the loan would be paid.

Even so, I had a little money to spare, enough to buy wallpaper for upstairs and paint for the kitchen. Catherine, Sarah, and Joseph came one Saturday and did the wallpapering. Even now I smile, remembering, almost hearing their laughter. My children, adults that they were, working—no, playing together. I see

Joseph, straddling the stairwell to hang the longest strips, Emily and Catherine recklessly brushing paste because Sarah said, "Too much is better than too little." I stayed out of the way, fixing lunch and listening to their talk.

The upstairs rooms looked fresh and bright. What I needed to do now was box up Emily's things that still remained in her dresser, under the bed, and around the house. She and Aaron would be home in a year unless Aaron decided to reenlist and, once they were settled someplace, she would want them.

I got some cartons from the garage and set to work. A sweater under the bed, mismatched socks in a drawer, leftover clothes from junior high school—it was amazing and entertaining to see what Emily had accumulated. I found an Elvis magazine behind the television downstairs, lipstick, and a toothbrush in the bathroom, boots by the back door, a necklace under a chair cushion. Finding the necklace made me think of Emily's ring and I went to my jewelry box to get it. Now would be a good time just to slip the ring in among her other things for her to find on her own. The ring was gone, no telling for how long. Without even thinking, I knew who had taken it. Cole, putting one more thing over. I sighed. Would there be no end to it?

Emily's belongings, seemingly small on their own, added up. And I kept finding things that had belonged to Cole. A cigarette lighter, lists of "relic" buyers, a tie. By the time I finished, four good-sized cartons were stacked in Emily's bedroom upstairs and two small cartons of Cole's things had been hauled to the garage. Maybe I should have just thrown them out, but it didn't seem right, somehow. The house was void of Emily reminders and Cole-leftovers, at least the material things. Sometimes there were still ghosts in the air making me lonely; a whiff of Cole's cigarette smoke, an echo of Emily's lighthearted laugh. I took the photo album from my desk and looked through it, wanting reminders of those people who shared my life, this house, for so many years—Catherine, Sarah, Joseph, Emily. And Cole.

I have never been one of those people who fill tables and walls with framed photos of babies turned into adults, weddings and birthdays, anniversaries and graduations. This was distraction, clutter, eventual uneasiness when memory couldn't recall the name of this or that baby. No, I wouldn't start now. The photo album went back into the desk. Looking and remembering were enough.

The downstairs rooms needed decorating, too. Feeling flush, and a little reckless, I hired a local woman to paper the living room and bedroom. I liked the result and decided to buy carpeting for the two rooms. Then the furniture looked a little shabby and I found a sofa that opened into a bed and bought that, just in case overnight guests showed up. Guests could sleep upstairs, of course, but there was no heat in the winter and stair-climbing didn't suit everyone. I was thinking of my sister, Connie. Maybe she would come visit.

I painted the bathroom myself—it was small, after all and I was tired of that pale green that seemed to show up everywhere. Now the room was a bright peach.

So Ma was right after all about hard work being the remedy for life's rough moments. I looked around my renovated home and smiled. I would be happy here.

My extravagance didn't end with redecorating. Now that I had more time to spend with my teacher friends, and more places to go, a new car was definitely needed. I had never owned a new car, always bought used, someone else's cast-off. *Why not buy a new one?*, I thought. Cole had never hesitated to buy new vehicles, even when his priorities should have been elsewhere.

Now I had my own priorities, the means to obtain them and no one to tell me I couldn't.

The car was a gleaming forget-me-not blue with four doors to make it easier for my teacher-passengers to enter and exit. Joseph shopped with me, pointing out all the good and bad points of the cars we looked at. I signed for the financing right at the car dealer's office, thinking how, a few years ago, no debt equaled no credit. Now, when I owed more money than I ever had owed in my life, my credit was golden.

Joseph told me that Cole and Velna were married and living in a trailer parked on a friend's farm. He laughed about it, saying that Velna had followed Cole from worksite to worksite until Cole hired her as office clerk in the work trailer. So her pursuit had been successful, after all. Mother Morgan used to say, when I was wishing for one thing or another, "Amy, beware your heart's desire," and I thought of those words now. How long before Velna's star would turn to tinsel? Velna's gas station, with its little attached apartment, had gone up for sale months ago, making it clear to me they wouldn't be living there. For that I was grateful, considering the few blocks that separated her property and mine.

I had mixed feelings about Cole's marriage. I was, surprisingly, sad, thinking that he was now gone from me forever. *Well, he's supposed to be,* I told myself, *that's what divorce is.* On the other hand, I was relieved, thinking that he would be Velna's problem now, and his attention diverted from thoughts or resentments tied to me. Maybe I was a little jealous, too, because Velna would now be my children's stepmother. Would there be family gatherings at Cole's and Velna's? *Not for a while,* I reminded myself, *too little room in Cole's house-trailer for that.*

One weeknight when I was correcting student papers at the kitchen table, there was a knock at the front door. I put my work aside and opened the door. It was a neighbor, a widower from up the block.

"I was walking out this evening and saw your light. Thought I'd stop and say hello. Can I come in?"

"Come in, Fred, I was just doing some work in the kitchen."

I wondered what he wanted. We were not friends and hadn't been friends even when his wife was alive. I had seen him loafing on the porch while his wife worked the garden, his disheveled appearance a sharp contrast to her tidy hair and crisp aprons.

Tonight he was dressed in suit and tie, even if the tie was crooked, a detail I couldn't help but notice after years of Cole's impeccable suits and ties. But of course there was no way Fred could replicate Cole's style, or looks, for that matter.

I considered offering Fred coffee.

"Nice place you have here, Miz Morgan. Looks like you been fixing her up some." He surveyed the wallpaper, carpet, and curtains. "Is the place paid for?"

I decided not to offer Fred coffee.

"Actually, no," I told him, trying to hide my irritation. "The divorce cost me a huge amount, and I owe so much I'll probably never get it paid for. Is your house paid for?"

"Well, uh, yes and no." He paused. I raised my eyebrows, looked at him directly and waited. The silence stretched…

"Guess I'll get along," he said, shifting from one foot to the other. "Just stopped to be neighborly. Good luck to you, Miz Morgan." And he sort of scurried to the door and disappeared.

Wife shopping. That's what Fred was up to. I laughed, thinking about it, and the more I thought about it the harder I laughed. Imagine, that old fool coming to my door looking for a housekeeper, cook, and washerwoman. Didn't he know I had just finished my turn with that? It would take more than a rusty man in a crooked tie to get my attention. Still, I had to admit I was cheered by the evening's events. I hadn't laughed so much in years.

Chapter Five

In no time at all another year rolled by and Christmas was closing in. Dinner would be at my place, home, and all the children would be there. Emily and Aaron had returned from Nebraska, found a little house nearby, and Emily was pregnant.

Joseph and Barbara were living in the basement of a house Joseph was building, with Cole's sometime help. Joseph's strength and weight had returned at an amazing pace, or so it seemed to me, and he had returned to work in the job Frank had offered. The house, he said, with room for their three boys, would be done by next summer.

Sarah and Emmett spent a lot of time working on the house they bought before Emily was married. They were thinking of adding a wing to provide bigger bedrooms for themselves and daughter.

Catherine and Tom had two children now, had moved to a bigger house not far from their earlier place, remaining more than an hour's drive away. Not so bad, I told myself, comparing it to past races to Ford hospital on the Lodge freeway.

So, six grandchildren and another coming. I was a grandmother, sure enough, a role I felt in name only. Except for Catherine's two, they were all within fifteen miles and I saw them occasionally, sometimes for an evening of babysitting. Ma always said there was a reason God gave babies to the young, and I knew now what she meant. These little people wore me out. I suppose I wasn't the typical grandmother, in that I was happy to deal with these youngsters in small, infrequent doses. I thought about that and decided it was all right. Mostly I thought of my children and if I could help them by babysitting, then that's what I would do.

I was happy to have my house filled again with the people I loved and the laughter they brought. Everyone brought food for Christmas dinner, and Sarah teased Joseph that dinner amounted to one huge potluck, knowing how Joseph always hated potluck dinners and would eat only foods brought from home. Joseph simply grinned and shook his head.

"It's not the same, Sarah," he said, "Everything here's home-made, just like you." That got a big laugh, a few comments and one or two playful pokes between adults-turned-children for a day.

After dinner, after food had been cleared and dishes washed, everyone gathered around the tree for gift opening. This sounds so ordinary, just telling it, and maybe it was, but it was filled with joy and happiness for me. What else is there but family, a place to put them, and food to share?

No one said a word about Cole.

When school resumed after Christmas break, there was a new poster on the bulletin board outside the principal's office. Della Robbins, one of my fellow teachers, pulled it down and brought it to the lunchroom where we gathered every day. She said someone had great nerve to just post such an advertisement at the school, undoubtedly without permission. It was true that postable items were highly restricted and those displayed had to be properly initialed by the principal or his secretary. There were no initials on this posting. But why all the fuss? What was the ad for? There was no hurrying Della into answering these questions—she was enjoying being the center of attention and was doing her best to create a moment of suspense.

Finally she unfolded the paper and four of us watched as she smoothed the poster on the table. It was a travel poster, only a travel poster, nothing more.

A series of Greyhound bus tours, some with interspersed air or rail travel, was being offered by a nearby travel agent. It was a series designed for teachers, built around school schedules and approved by the Michigan Education Association. That tidbit might account for the poster's unmolested presence on the bulletin board.

Della said that this might be a fun way to add credits to our teaching credentials, maybe even get a tax deduction. What did we think?

I looked at the destinations offered: New York City, Boston, Nashville, Las Vegas, New Orleans, Hawaii.

"We need more information," I said. "One of us should look into this, get costs, what the tours really cover, and other details. Nashville or New Orleans would suit me, if they're not too expensive."

The other women agreed and so it was that Della was selected to research possibilities. She wrote down the phone number from the poster and said she would pin it back up on the bulletin board. "Maybe others will be interested too," she said, smiling. This was a nice attitude change from a half-hour earlier.

That summer, six of us took the Nashville tour, one of the least expensive and closest to home. Most of us had done little traveling on our own, if at all, and being with our own little group was reassuring. The entire bus was teachers, as we should have expected, some in groups and some on their own. Most had notebooks and cameras and talked about "enrichment studies," their nerves or digestive processes, and whether the beds in the hotels would be conducive to sleep. I kept my thoughts to myself, a lifetime habit not easily discarded. Our group had been assigned three rooms at the Nashville hotel, and we had already decided who would share each room. I was with Della, and that was fine with me. Four of us were single, over fifty. The other two were married women, about forty, and they paired together.

I guess everyone who goes to Nashville sees the Grand Old Opry, and we did. The crowds, the colorful lights, the air of excitement and the energetic shows were exhilarating and mood lifting. During these days, I became aware that the air around me was becoming lighter, brighter. Something dark was unwinding and being taken away, almost like silk is unwound from a silkworm's cocoon. I felt happier, uplifted and giddy. I kept the wonder of this experience to myself, lest it evaporate under the glare of acknowledgment.

Della and I got along quite well as roommates, not the case for some of the group. Complaints began at breakfast and drifted in the air throughout the day. "She takes so long to shower." "There's just no room on the sink for my things, she has so many jars and bottles." "Who'd have thought she'd snore that loudly?" If the trip had been longer, I no doubt would have heard the same grumbling from all. Human nature, I suppose, that everyone's troubles invariably arise from the other person's shortcomings.

I still felt lighter after the Greyhound carried us home and summer stretched before me again. Della had enjoyed the tour, too, her first ever trip outside of Michigan, and we vowed to take more excursions together.

"We need the enrichment," I said, and Della laughed. We both laughed, a sign, I suppose, that we had been enriched in some small way.

Chapter Six

I first met Will Carter when his three children were students at my last rural school. He was a local farmer and active member of the school board who visited school regularly, usually with his wife. He said it was his duty to inspect the facility, and I suppose that was true but he was also spying on my teaching, the way Pa used to do when he was a director. Actually, Will reminded me of Pa in many ways. He was soft-spoken, mannerly, and never harsh. His inquiries were polite and when I requested supplies or repairs, they were promptly furnished. If someone was going to oversee my workplace, I was glad it was the Carters and not certain others.

Since the rural school had closed, and I began teaching in town, I rarely saw Will Carter. He came to school events until his children graduated and then, I supposed, just returned to his farm. Soon after, I was surprised to hear that his and his wife had divorced.

Some months later, Will Carter telephoned. He was full of small talk and, just when I began to wonder what he really wanted, he invited me to dinner. He even asked where I would like to go, and I politely deferred to his judgment, as I thought I should.

He took me to a wonderful steak restaurant in Lansing, a place I had driven past many times, admiring its elegance and imagining just how expensive such a place might be. The evening was most enjoyable, and the food was, indeed, expensive. I found myself relaxing in his easy presence, warmed by his company.

Will was, I thought, a handsome man, not in the stylish, flashy way that Cole was handsome, but handsome in an understated, comfortable way, a lot like Pa dressed up for Sunday services. You might say that if Cole's style was defined by his green sharkskin suits and Florsheims, Will's was defined by gray wool flannel and well-worn oxfords.

When Will took me home, he walked me to the door, planted a brotherly kiss on my cheek and said "good night." I hoped he would call again and said so. He smiled and said he would.

My head was spinning with possibilities. Trips, evenings, weekends…

Friday evenings soon became our night together, then Sunday our day. Sometimes we went out—never to bars, which Will decried—but to fine restaurants and eateries around Lansing. Sometimes I cooked at home. Will invited me to his farm where he would cook dinner.

The Carter farm was less than a mile from the school where I had taught. The house was smaller than most area farm houses, but larger than my own house. Dairy cattle filled the barns and chickens were contained behind wire. Only the ducks were allowed free range. It was easy to see that Will's farm was his pride and joy—in its freshly painted barns, straight standing fences, clean machinery neatly aligned in sheds and barns.

The house was tidy, well-maintained and smelled of coffee and furniture polish. Will cooked omelettes and served them alongside toasted bread, fresh sliced tomatoes and canned peaches.

I couldn't remember the last time, if ever, that anyone had cooked a meal especially for me. I must say I was a bit bedazzled.

So, when Christmas came around again, it was natural to invite Will to the family dinner. It was at Sarah's this year and her little house seemed to overflow with people, noise, and laughter. I could see the children giving Will the once-over, but he didn't seem to notice and was his usual affable self, seeming to enjoy the celebration as much as I did.

The month after, Will asked me to marry him. I shouldn't have been surprised, I suppose, but I was. I liked our arrangement as it was, saw no need for marriage, and told him so.

"The farm needs a woman, and I need a wife," he told me, in a voice a little firmer than was his custom. I looked away.

"I'll take good care of you," he said, taking my hand. "You won't have to teach anymore, the farm earns more than enough for anything either of us needs."

"My house…" I began, but he interrupted.

"You can sell your house. It'll give us a good nest egg for travel, whatever we decide to do, Amy. We can have your children and mine and their families every year for Christmas…you know there's plenty of room. What do you say?"

"I don't know, Will, I…" Actually, I was dumbstruck, shocked by the ideas he tossed into the air so easily, so well-rehearsed. *Quit teaching? Sell my house?*

"Amy, I need an answer. We've been seeing each other for months now, and it's time. I'm a traditional man, and I need to be married. What it boils down to is this: either you marry me or I marry someone else. What will your answer be?"

"Someone else? You have someone else?" His words were a knife to my heart.

"I didn't say that, Amy. What I meant is that I intend to marry. If not you, I'll find another. I don't mean to sound harsh, Amy, but that's the simple truth."

He stood from the couch where we had been sitting together and turned toward the door.

"Tuesday, Amy. Call me by Tuesday if you change your mind."

And he left, just walked away, not even a goodnight kiss.

I thought about his words all day Sunday. I asked myself whether I could give up teaching now, with only a few more years until retirement. I had worked hard for more than twenty seasons, knowing I was building a pension that would support my later years. If I didn't need the money to live on, as Will said, it was still the reward for those years, a sort of pot of gold at the end of the rainbow. I didn't want to just throw it away. If I didn't give up teaching, there was the driving to consider. In winter the roads were often treacherous and I dreaded having to drive them again. That aside, it sounded to me that, for Will, my continuing to teach was not an option.

What rankled the most was Will's presumption that my house would be "our" nest egg, mere nickels and dimes to be squandered on travel or other whimsy. He was mentally disposing of my assets as his right, never mind that my ideas might be different. Here were ghosts from the past—Cole claiming our joint tax refunds for himself—Pa selling the house at Crane without talking about it. If I did what Will wanted and the marriage didn't work out, I would be left in the lurch. Nowhere to go, no money to buy a place. The more I thought about it, the more resentful I became.

And then there was the idea that "the farm needs a woman." I thought of Pa's farm, when Ma was sick and gone to Traverse City, and all the work that fell to me during that time. I thought of Ma, worn thin and working faster and faster to keep up with the endless cycles of farm seasons with their hatching chicks, new lambs, gardens and canning… I could see Ma still, hair falling over one eye as she filled jars with boiling fruit from a kettle on the stove, "If you ever think of being a farm wife, Amy," she was saying, "Ever think of owning a farm, just remember one thing. You don't own the farm, the farm owns you."

Will had shown another side of himself, a "take charge" side where his word trumped any ace I might hold. Like Pa, and I dreaded saying it, but I could finally see it, bending everything and everyone toward his own ends.

If only Will could have at least said that he cared for me. If saying he loved me was too much, I would have welcomed lesser words. I would have welcomed his expression of affection, hopefully an affection deep enough and strong enough to carry us through these last decades of our lives.

A thought picture, un-summoned, popped into my mind. The widower, Fred, from up the street, coming to my door wife shopping. I could see that Will was not so different, simply presenting himself with better grooming and finer manners. I should have seen it sooner.

It took me two days to think it through. I would not give up my career for a man. I would not give up my house for a farmer. I would not give up my freedom for a new master.

I thought of Will once, on Tuesday, while sharing lunch with Della in the school lunchroom, but I didn't telephone him.

In less than six months Will married a widow from his township, a woman whose children I had also taught at the nearby school.

Chapter Seven

The next summer I took another Greyhound tour, this time to New Orleans. Later there were trips to Boston, Las Vegas, and Hawaii, the latter being my first airplane trip and a thrilling one at that. The trips were adventures and enlightening in unexpected ways. Enlightening because, as a teacher, I knew that students learned history best when history was "kept alive." Just try comparing words on a dry page to spending midnight amidst the revelry and excitement of the New Orleans French Quarter.

Everywhere I traveled, I waited and watched. I hoped that, among all these people, there might be just one man who would choose me as a friend, companion, and wife. I learned that most of the men in our travel groups were married, or at least firmly attached to their travel mates. The few who were friendly and available seemed sub-standard, somehow, like stray puppies who might follow you home if encouraged. I have never been a fan of strays.

Hawaii was a thrilling place to visit, with its luxury hotels, parties, luaus, and tours to beaches, volcanoes, and extraordinary landscapes. There was little doubt I could have found a companion here; smiling men and women of all ages wended through the crowds at every event. Some would sit at your table with the tiniest encouragement. Later, I would laugh at how put off I was by these "social practices," recognizing my reaction as reflective of early values. The truths that I knew then remained. To put it simply, I am not a companion-for-the-evening sort. Hawaii was no exception. I was not on vacation from reality.

After Hawaii, I more or less resigned myself to singlehood. My own home, freedom to come and go, simple peace and qui-et—these outweighed whatever a warm body might offer on a cold winter night. Looking back, I could see that when I had said "no" to Will, had refused to bend towards his wishes, something in me had permanently shifted.

"Bend or break," Ma had warned me, and it seemed I had spent my whole life bending. Suddenly, when I finally refused to bend, nothing in me fractured. In fact, I felt more whole, more like myself, and I sensed that some of the parts twisted by all that bending had begun to heal.

Emily telephoned to invite me for coffee at the house she and Aaron had bought north of town. Catherine and Sarah were coming, she said, and she hoped I could make it. She knew I would. Anytime my children offered time with me, I took it, if only to share their worries and listen to stories about their growing families.

The "coffee" turned out to be a news conference of sorts. Sarah had filed for divorce.

I listened while Sarah talked, her sisters asked questions, and she responded. Sometimes everyone talked at once, that was their way, and it was hard to follow, but I listened. It sounded to me as if Sarah had just gotten tired of Emmett. I could see how that would happen, but how many married couples could say the same? Fatigue seemed like small grounds for divorce.

"We'll be fine," Sarah insisted. "Emmett is being real good about the kids and the house." As an aside, she added, "Not that he has a choice." She laughed, but the words bore the stamp of truth.

"I've turned my thoughts toward finding a better job." Sarah added. "Not that I don't like my job, I just mean one that pays more money."

"What kind of jobs have you applied for?" Catherine asked, and Sarah's reply was not very satisfying.

"None. I'm thinking, concentrating on attracting an opportunity with my thoughts. Of course I'm telling everyone I know, and with my talent…"

We all laughed then and I just shook my head.

I had mixed feelings about Sarah's decision. Down deep, I still thought marriage was the best way and there were lots worse men in the world than Emmett. Even so, here I was, single. Maybe if I had divorced earlier, like Sarah…well, I wasn't going to get lost in that. Sarah had made up her mind and that's the way it would be. Her two children were no longer babies, but I just knew she would be needing my help babysitting more than ever.

It was that same year that Joseph told me Barbara had moved out of the house they had worked so hard to build together. Maybe the same boredom that caught up with Sarah had moved Barbara to run off with the carpenter Joseph had hired to build a garage. The difference was that Sarah would be all right. Joseph was crushed.

I knew that the whole family would miss Barbara, the spark of her personality, her audacious outspokenness and the steadfast carry-through she had shown during Joseph's illness. Oh, I had less charitable thoughts, too, but they were aimed mostly at the carpenter.

There was little I could do except be available for conversation and babysitting and that's what I did.

Wolffton schools introduced a new program to "improve" the quality of education, as if that was a new concept. As it turned out, this meant not renewing contracts for older teachers, like me. Not that the word "older" was spoken—we had become more sensitized to age discrimination and other preferences since the LBJ years, but that's what was meant. "More experienced, more highly paid" teachers would be replaced by a new generation of teachers fresh from college and eager to imprint modernized curricula on impressionable minds. No need to worry about the "older" teachers, the argument went. They would have their pensions and social security.

I was sixty-four when this plan was announced. You can say that I would have retired in another year anyway, and that's probably true, but the idea stuck in my craw. It seemed little to ask that I be allowed to make the decision myself, keep my dignity, maybe have a little luncheon to celebrate, instead of someone just lowering the boom on me and my fellow teachers all at the same time.

There were no special incentives or bonuses being offered in exchange for our gracious exit, only the same pensions and health benefits we would have received had we volunteered to retire. We would go quietly, my colleagues and I, without protest, bargaining or questions. *Of course*, I told myself, *women of my generation don't confront, don't protest.* Della summed up her perspective one day at lunch. "Yesterday we were just old hens," she said. "Today we're lame ducks."

Once I got over initial resentments, I was surprised to find that retirement was a great relief and blessing. No more alarm clock, no more paperwork piled high on the table every night. I had long-since paid off my car and Cole's share of the house. Money, the number one issue looming in my mind, turned out to be less of an issue than I had feared. I was out of debt, on my own, with a promised income that required no work. If I'd have thought about that when I was twenty-five, it would have sounded like Utopia. A modest Utopia, perhaps, but a Utopia nonetheless.

My sister Connie came to visit now and then and slept on the hide-a-bed in the living room. I read books and watched movies on TV. There was ample time to fill in with grand-parenting duties. I took up quilt-making and eventually stitched quilts for my daughters, son, and ten grandchildren.

An invitation came for a fiftieth wedding anniversary party for Connie and Wes. "A time for celebration" the invitation said, "You are invited to join in…" The event struck too many painful chords for me.

Cole and I had stood up with Connie and Wes, just months before our own marriage. I couldn't bear it if a photo was planned of the original bridal party. Cole and Velna would undoubtedly be there, I the third party, odd wife out. I had attended events before when Cole was there, weddings mostly, but some family gatherings of various sorts. Cole inevitably would corner me to drag up some past injustice—to him, of course. The more he talked, the louder his voice, until I would just shrink in my shoes and wish I were elsewhere.

After a few of these episodes, I told Catherine, Sarah, Joseph, and Emily that I would no longer attend any event if Cole was invited. I didn't want to miss out on events in my children's lives, but I had to put an end to this. So if I stayed home once in awhile when I could have gone out? As I had told myself before, *sometimes there are worse things than being alone.*

As it turned out, I couldn't convince myself that missing Connie's party was right. I bought a new dress, had my hair done and put on a happy face. When I walked in, the hall was full of family and friends, young and old, and Cole and Velna were the center of attention. Cole was holding forth, talking and gesturing amid an audience of appreciative listeners. I might as well have been invisible for all the attention I got.

I signed the book and Connie, seeing me, broke away to say hello. She laughed her tinkling laugh while telling me that Wes's sister-in-law was crying because her own husband had died and they, too, would have been married fifty years. So sad. Not a word for me, who might have been married fifty years myself, as Connie well knew.

I wondered whether living those additional years with Cole would have been worth it. So I was very unhappy then. I might have been able to hang on. I had my work and after awhile things didn't hurt quite so much. I would have liked to be the center of attention at a party like this.

After awhile things don't hurt so much? What's all this misery about then? Who are you kidding? Before I could answer these self-imposed questions, Cole came walking over with Velna at his side.

"Amy, so you did show up. Joseph said you might not."

"Connie's my sister," I said.

"There's something I want to talk to you about," Cole began. I clenched my teeth, wondering what it would be this time.

"The gate-leg, Amy. I never did pick it up and I'm thinking I should. I can bring the pick-up next week-end…"

I wasn't going to listen to this.

"No, Cole, that table, the gate-leg, is mine."

"You want to argue here at your sister's party? You know I wanted it. I told you. I bought it, remember? It belongs to me." His voice was beginning to rise.

I turned and walked out of the hall onto the veranda. Cole followed.

"After all these years, Cole? How many times have you brought this up? Read your court papers. The table is listed as mine. The matter was settled nearly two decades ago."

"I'll buy it then." Cole lowered his voice a little. "I can give you cash." There were a half-dozen people on the porch now, including Connie's son.

"Come on, Uncle Cole," he said, "We want to hear the rest of that story about the revenuers coming to your door."

Cole allowed himself to be led back into the hall and the other guests followed. Velna, who had not said a word, gave me a look before turning to follow.

"Velna." She turned back toward me. "Just one thing. Tell Cole the gate-leg's not for sale," I spat the words at her. "Not today, not ever."

"I'll tell him tomorrow," she said, before walking back into the hall.

PART FIVE

The Clock Winds Down

The next day, thinking about my encounter with Cole, I was a little ashamed of the way I had popped off to Velna. She hadn't done anything, unless you count chasing my then-husband across five counties. But that was ancient history, he was hers, now, and heaven help her.

Leaves were falling from the apple trees as I watched through my kitchen window. It would soon be winter again and I didn't mind. My car could stay in the garage, ample food was in the cupboard, and I had money to pay Consumers Power to keep the place warm. Just being warm and fed were blessings I was thankful for every day, recalling those many winters when my bones seemed filled with ice and food portions were weighted toward Cole and the children.

I heard the thump of the daily newspaper hitting the front porch and watched the newsboy wheel on up the street on his bicycle. News of the world, or at least the state and county, delivered daily for my convenience, just one example of how self-indulgent my life had become. Sometimes I didn't even read the newspaper, simply turned to Ann Landers and the crossword puzzle. Other times I read the obituaries, looking for names I knew and seeing them more often every year. Some days I would pen a note to the editor, just to set him straight on word usage or poor grammar in one article or another. Some of the gaffs I read would have earned the dunce cap from this fifth-grade teacher and I was sure that this newspaper editor had been no student of mine.

Today I just let the newspaper lay where it had fallen and poured myself another cup of coffee. As so often happened, my thoughts turned to the lives of my children.

At Sarah's urging, that is to say, she practically dragged him out of his house, Joseph accompanied Sarah to a Parents Without Partners meeting in Lansing. Joseph had been unhappy and at loose ends ever since Barbara had left and, although he went to work every day, he just didn't seem to be able to stir up his social life. Sarah, I thought wryly, was taking Joseph "wife-shopping." I wondered whether she might be "husband-shopping," herself, but after one meeting, she dropped out, leaving Joseph on his own.

Surprisingly, Joseph continued with the group and, after a while, met Karen, a divorcee with one daughter somewhat younger than Joseph's own boys. Karen seemed pleasant enough, eager to make a good impression. Soon I had another daughter-in-law and one more granddaughter.

As for Sarah, she had "attracted" the job she wanted and was more wrapped up in her career than anything else. Emmett had promptly remarried, snagged by a woman with several children, a discarded spouse and a house. For herself, Sarah disparaged husband-shopping or "doing the bar scene" in favor of esoterically "attracting" the right man, as she had with her job. I didn't say that she might have to wait a long time, seeing how slow the universe moves. Meanwhile, she went out when asked, often I suspected with married men. The advantage of dating married men, she once told me, was that they usually went home at night.

Catherine and Tom bought a home closer by, now that both had retired and their children were grown. Both preferred the open space that a more rural community offered and were more than ready to leave the hustle and bustle of city life.

I could count on Emily to stop by every few days and these were always mood lifters for me. Sometimes we shopped together, although the malls were proving more and more tiring. Soon I would give them up altogether and just shop one store at a time, or by catalog. Emily shopped for me on occasion, always willing to fill my meager grocery lists, and I came to rely on her for that.

I mused how I relied on my children for different things. Emily, closest by, was the one I saw the most. I could depend on her for day-to-day errands, company, food treats from her kitchen and even bed-checks. She added a welcome element of security to my days.

Joseph was always there if something needed fixing and to keep me posted on his ever-improving health. He would drop by just to check on things or to tell me about his sons and their lives. Sometimes he brought news of Cole's life, stories I relished for various reasons. I felt very fortunate, not only that Joseph was alive and well, but that he had, unbidden, taken charge of automobile and home maintenance. I also was pleased that, with Karen, his life had taken a happier turn.

Sarah was my tax, business, and paperwork resource. She said she liked researching tax and legal issues and so I left these to her. If I had a grievance, as I sometimes did, with bills, the bank or service providers, a word to Sarah brought enough commotion down on their heads to resolve the problem. Effort that loomed as difficult for me seemed easy to her. I did love hearing the resulting stories, too.

Catherine, with her medical training, was my first medical resource. If I had a health concern, I telephoned Catherine and her advice was always good. She went with me to doctor appointments, quizzed me on my prescriptions and diet and listened to my concerns.

You might say I had an Advisory Committee that supported me in all areas of my life.

Over the years, Catherine, Sarah, Joseph, and Emily had each asked me about Cole, a variety of questions that covered their lifetimes, and yet one question was always the same, "Why did you stay married so long?"

So many reasons, mostly vague, fragmented or irrational, had come to mind over the years but the thoughts had never coalesced into anything definitive. If I couldn't clearly answer that question for myself, how could I answer it for them?

I fashioned an indirect response, a dodge, perhaps, but nonetheless true. I told each one, "I don't know the answer but this I do know…if I hadn't stayed, then I wouldn't have you."

I felt fortunate, indeed.

For my seventy-seventh birthday, Sarah invited me out to dinner. Well, it wasn't just Sarah, it was also Jim, a man she had met six months earlier when he was hired at the company where she worked. Sarah insisted her concentration and focus after all these years had worked again. She said he was divorced, city born and bred, a college graduate and Roman Catholic by birth and training. All that was fine and dandy but what alarmed me most was that Jim had moved into Sarah's place. This wasn't like Sarah at all…during her years of singleness she had never had a live-in male friend. I worried about his background, almost by definition that "city slicker" that Cole, Father Morgan and his father before him, had warned feminine family members against. This dinner would be the first time I had laid eyes on Jim.

Jim drove us to a favored restaurant while Sarah and I talked. Or I should say, Sarah talked. I remained apprehensive and didn't say much. By mid-dinner, however, it was clear to me that Jim was not the feared city slicker.

Throughout my life I had not tried to influence my children's choice of partner. My opinions, some of which are voiced in earlier pages, I kept to myself. But now, the idea that Jim had moved in with Sarah without the benefit of marriage was on my mind. The thought rankled. That's the only explanation I can come up with for the question I asked between the main course and dessert.

"What are your intentions regarding my daughter?"

"Mother!" Sarah sounded as if she couldn't believe her ears. I kept my eyes on Jim.

He seemed thoughtful, slightly amused or non-plussed. Now Sarah was looking at him too. He was not the least put off.

"I'm going to marry her," were the words he spoke just before they brought the cake and ice cream dessert.

Sarah told me later that this was the first she'd heard about marriage. Jim hadn't proposed to her nor had they spoken of marriage. Now the die was cast and they were married months later.

Chapter Two

Winter came and winter went, and I marked Memorial Day on my calendar. Catherine, Sarah and Emily would go with me to visit Ma's and Pa's graves at Poseyville, as I had done for years. Connie usually went with me but now she said she didn't feel comfortable driving to my house and back home again. The freeways were too busy, she said, the traffic made her nervous. For once, we were on the same page, my sister and I. Freeways bothered me too, and even though the trip to Poseyville was not freeway driving, I didn't want to drive alone. Besides, I drove less and less since a fender bender had shaken my confidence a few years back. My car sat in the garage now, mostly unused. When I shared my thoughts with Emily, she called the others. I offered to buy lunch.

Sarah drove her car, Catherine sat in front and I sat in back with Emily. As the three of them talked, I watched the scenery race by, familiar and yet new, fields of green or freshly turned brown stretching further as we went north.

"Oh, oh," Sarah interrupted herself, "I don't remember this road being gravel."

She had missed a turn while I was watching the scenery instead of watching the route. Good thing I hadn't driven the road by myself. It was also a good thing that the paved road had turned to gravel. Otherwise, who knew how many miles out of the way Sarah would have driven? Now she just turned the car around and we zipped back to the corner we should have taken.

We left flowers on the graves and drove into Midland to see my brother, Davis, and his wife, Genevieve. Davis was in a nursing home now and we drove directly there. Genevieve would be waiting. I knew Davis had suffered a stroke some months earlier and believed that he was recovering and able to speak. This expectation did not prepare me for what I saw. Davis lay in bed, under neatly folded and smooth sheets, a mannequin in a store-window bed. His eyes were closed, a tube was in his nose, others under the covers.

"Your sister's here," Genevieve said close to his face. "Amy's here with her girls."

Davis neither opened his eyes nor spoke. He never moved, not even to breathe, it seemed. *He's better off dead*, I thought, just before Genevieve said, "He's alive, our Davis is alive, thanks to the feeding tube. He is still with me, praise Jesus."

I bit my tongue.

"Go ahead, Amy, touch his hand," Genevieve urged. "He knows you're here. His hand is warm. Say something, we think he hears us."

I reached out briefly and then withdrew my hand. I couldn't bring myself to touch what remained of my brother. He lay before me, a fleshy lump smaller than real life, viable only as a laboratory experiment, not dead but not alive either. It was just too horrific. I hoped Genevieve was wrong and that Davis didn't know I was there or how strongly I was repulsed. I couldn't speak, couldn't touch his still warm hand. I sensed panic rising in my throat, wanted to leave, and Emily, seeing my distress, made some excuse and walked me out to the car.

On the trip home, Catherine fumed about medicine and religion being twisted into fruitless consequences while Sarah listened and drove and Emily sat quietly beside me. Perhaps my fate would be worse, but it would not be like Davis's. I had signed, notarized papers that said so.

When we got home, and I went to get out of the car, Catherine remarked that my ankles were swollen.

"Your legs don't usually swell this way, do they?" she asked.

"No, but sometimes. It's nothing."

"It's something, Mother. I want you to call your doctor and make an appointment. I'll drive you. We shouldn't ignore this."

That was Catherine, my medical advisor daughter. After I was safely inside the house, she, Sarah and Emily said their goodbyes and headed home. I would call the doctor in the morning.

The day had been tiring for me and I just skipped supper and sank into the soft comfort of my living room chair. Catherine had scolded me months before for skipping meals and had brought a supply of nutritional drinks.

"If you can't fix yourself something," she said, "At least drink one of these. You need the vitamins and minerals."

I had agreed, but tonight just couldn't make myself get up, go to the refrigerator, retrieve a can and open it. I was thinking about Davis.

The schoolhouse clock on my living room wall was ticking louder than usual. I watched the pendulum swing its small, lazy arc while the minutes passed. I thought of Connie missing today's trip.

I had always believed that Connie led a pampered life. She was spoiled as a child, flattered and applauded as a young woman, and indulged by an attentive husband who catered to her wishes. Her whole life seemed a frivolous party. And yet, she had lost Wes to cancer not too long after their fiftieth wedding anniversary party. I visited Wes once or twice at the hospital when Connie quit going. She said it was too painful for her, she just couldn't bear to see him like that.

"Selfish to the end," I had thought, remembering my own struggles during Joseph's illness. The resolve and endurance that kept me going then weren't with me at Davis's bedside today. I had been repelled by my brother's appearance and condition. I wanted to deny or escape the dreadfulness of his existence. Was my reaction so different from Connie's reaction to Wes's last illness?

A mere four years later, Connie also lost her only son, Wes, Jr. to cancer. She had since moved from her home into an apartment somewhat smaller than her house had been.

A few years ago I shared some of my feelings with Connie. We were reminiscing and I meant to clear the air of these old cobwebs. Instead, she gave me some of the hardest words I ever heard her speak. Her rebuke was like shards of glass that cut even today.

"My husband's dead, my only son is dead, my house is gone. I have to watch every penny. Yes, I'm so lucky. Want to change places with me?"

I never wanted to change places with Connie. I can see, now, how my opinions and resentments got in the way of a full sisterly relationship. What I saw as her pampered life and shallow views, combined with my simmering resentment and self-centeredness, created a witch's brew of misunderstanding. I always knew that Connie had no comprehension of the life I led. Now I know that that I had no real comprehension of hers. Maybe she was the lucky one then. Maybe I am the lucky one now.

While these thoughts busy my mind, I watch the pretty wallpaper in my living room fade to gray. It reminds me of the washed out walls at Father Morgan's farm, where Cole and his brother squared off, where my piano was destroyed.

Cole. My years have never been free of Cole. I still thrill at recalling his good looks, great laugh, and the happy times we had at first. I think of Sunday drives, family outings rare enough to stand out like jewels in this necklace of years. I think, too, of

Cole's angry outbursts, his lawlessness, his chasing. His cruelty to our children.

Cole has never been called to account for any of it. Even when he fired his shotgun into the backside of a trespasser at his and Velna's place, he walked free, chastised only by a warning from sheriff's deputies. This story was told by Joseph, who laughed and made a joke about his father being untouchable.

Cole had been attacked by more than one irate husband, engaged in more brawls than one might count, and saw stars when racial name-calling brought him an ax handle to the head. He crashed cars, stood against union organizers with clubs, hustled pool players, left a man for dead, and, one way or another, made other people's property his own. His legacy of "enhanced" Indian relics may never be unraveled. Justice remains un-served.

Pastor would say that it is not my place to ask for, or seek vengeance. I hear the word *poison* in my mind and know that the emotion of these memories, played again and again, is killing me. I become aware that my jaw is set hard against my teeth. I take a deep breath and feel the twilight in the darkening room.

How many times have I tried to forgive Cole? Uncounted times, the answer goes. The Lord knows I believe in forgiveness, but where is it? I listen to my exhaled breathing and feel my jaw relax.

"I forgive you, Cole," I say aloud. "I forgive it all. I am dying under the weight of it."

I repeat the words of my resolve, my prayer, over and over, crowding the still air in the room with syllables. The wordy air spins round my head. In the long stillness, the only sound is my clock, ticking, ticking.

Gradually, ever so slowly, I feel a loosening in my shoulders. The leaden cloak of bitterness and anger that has lain there for decades begins to lift. Its weight rises, fades into dust, and floats away. When the burden is finally gone, I sit up straighter, press my back into the chair and take a deep breath. I open my eyes to a room that seems suddenly brighter, cleaner. The rosy pink of the wallpaper is as it should be.

I am finally free. I know I am free.

———————————

I have been going through my papers, books, and other things I have collected over the years, making lists. I do not want a lifetime of things to be tossed helter-skelter when I am gone. I have made lists before, changed them, changed my mind, or given whatever it was to the one who needed or admired it. This time I mean it.

The formal papers are long since done, as I have said before. These lists are just the personal things, dishes and jewelry, gifts from the children and from students. I have valued them, kept them, looked at them. They don't mean so much now, and as I make my lists I think of a poem Henry Wadsworth Longfellow wrote and called *Nature*. I copied its words from a textbook long ago. It suits me now:

As a fond mother when the day is o'er,
Leads by the hand her little child to bed,
Half willing, half reluctant to be led,
And leave his broken playthings on the floor,
Still gazing at them through the open door,
Nor wholly reassured and comforted
By promises of others in their stead,
Which, though more splendid, may not please him more;
So Nature deals with us, and takes away
Our playthings one by one, and by the hand
Leads us to rest so gently, that we go
Scarce knowing if we wish to go or stay,
Being too full of sleep to understand
How far the unknown transcends the what we know.

—*Henry Wadsworth Longfellow*

I am giving up my toys, some of them anyway. The car, a most important toy, sits in the garage. I still have the stereo that plays 45's and, although Emily has taken most of the Elvis records, I have kept a few. I stack them on the spindle and they begin to play as I put my lists and papers into the box marked Sarah. She will take care of what needs to be done when the time comes and I do not intend to look at paperwork again.

Elvis is asking *Are You Lonesome Tonight?* as I settle back in my chair and listen. Even Elvis is gone now, victim of that pernicious modern killer called fame. He left his music. I leave my lists.

This is the last time I will write. I am done.

Amelia Lorraine Whitlock Morgan

1907 – 1994

S